Free State Kit

Allergy-Friendly Cookbook

Vegan Foods Without Gluten, Wheat, Soy, Nuts, Dairy, or Eggs

Dawn Hamilton

Copyright © 2012 Dawn Hamilton.

All rights reserved. Except as permitted under U.S. Copyright Act of 1976, no part of this publication may be reproduced, distributed, or transmitted in any form or by any means, or stored in a database or retrieval system, without the prior written permission of the author.

Library of Congress Cataloging-in-Publication Data

ISBN-13: 978-1478274858

ISBN-10: 1478274859

Published in the United States of America
Free State Press, Inc., Lawrence, Kansas.

Editorial services by Clarissa Clarke

Cover photo courtesy of Meredith Kennedy of MK Designs

The recipes and information contained in this book are not intended to substitute competent medical advice. Those with multiple food allergies or other health concerns should speak with their healthcare provider before making any dietary changes. The publisher, author, Free State Kitchen and Bakery, and Free State Press, Inc., cannot be held responsible for any reactions resulting from our recipes, consuming products from our recommended suppliers, or accidental exposure to cross-contamination from non-approved suppliers.

First Edition

Table of Contents

Introduction
Living in the Free State

Welcome to living in the Free State, where you control what you eat and how good it tastes! For those of you who purchased our first book Free *State Bakery's Nothing to Sneeze At*, thank you for joining us again.

From today on, you will take back your power and enjoy eating some of your favorite comfort foods you thought you had to give it, and you'll be proud to share the extras (if you have any) with everyone else.

You may be looking at our subtitle and thinking vegan food that also contains no wheat, gluten, eggs, dairy, nuts, or soy- what exactly are we going to cook with? Good question! I will introduce you to gluten-free whole grains and flours, seeds, fruits, vegetables, and beans, that when prepared with some awesome allergy-friendly cheeses, sauces, and condiments really taste delicious, are nutritious, and feed your body and soul.

This entire book, from cover to cover, is catered to you, the person who has Celiac disease, wheat allergies, lactose intolerance, high cholesterol, or those unable or unwilling to eat eggs, nuts, soy, or animal products of any kind. Learning to locate and work with different grains, dairy and milk substitutes, and choosing brands that are conscious of what we put into our bodies is the key to having your food freedom again. It will also enliven your spirit, put a glow in your skin and eyes, and do something good for the planet.

Cooking with any restriction can be tricky, but I have taken all the guesswork out of it for you. I spent years perfecting each and every recipe, because this is how I need to eat, and believe me, I love to cook and eat. Here in this book I have plenty of quick cooking tasty foods, such as macaroni and cheese, that are kid tested by some of the most sensitive and picky eaters imaginable.

For those of you following along who are outside of the United States, I have added a metric conversion chart starting on page 154 to help you with measurements and temperatures.

Dawn Hamilton

Foods for Your Pantry
What to Use, and Where to get them

Agar Powder-a natural gelatin that is prepared from several species of red algae. It has high gelling properties, and used by vegetarians because true gelatin is made from calf's feet.

Agave Nectar-a liquid sweetener obtained from a cactus that is suitable for diabetics and is low on the glycemic index. Agave is a great alternative to honey for vegans. I love Wholesome Sweeteners brand **www.wholesomesweeteners.com**

Amaranth-is an ancient grain that is gluten-free and high in protein. Avoid if cross-contamination from nut flours could affect your health unless clearly labeled as safe. Get amaranth flour by Bob's Red Mill **www.bobsredmill.com**

Apple Cider Vinegar- Bragg's is my favorite brand by far, but any brand of raw, unpasteurized apple cider vinegar that still contains the "mother" (culture) is acceptable. These vinegars may appear cloudy due to the presence of the mother, but this is actually a good thing. Purchase online at **www.bragg.com**

Arrowroot-a gluten-free powder that is a great starch to use in baking and cooking. Avoid if cross-contamination from nut flours could affect your health unless clearly labeled as nut-free. I like Bob's **www.bobsredmill.com**

Baking powder-comes in two varieties, regular and double-acting. In some recipes, I specify the double-acting variety, as it seems to help give more lift to some gluten-free items. Look specifically for gluten-free on the label. Brands to look for- Rumson and Clabbergirl which are readily available in most supermarkets, but for the most allergic, Ener-G foods is the best supplier **www.ener-g.com**

Baking soda-often used in conjunction with baking powder in gluten-free baking, baking soda is a great leavening agent. So, if you see a recipe asking for both, it is not an error. Any brand will do but for the most allergic, Ener-G foods is the best supplier **www.ener-g.com**

Beans come in numerous varieties, and are loaded with protein and other trace minerals. You can purchase them dry and soak them, or purchase many varieties in cans or boxes, which is preferred because many cans contain BPA which can leech into the food. It is highly suggested you rinse canned beans well before adding to most recipes, just as we recommend discarding soaking water and cooking them in fresh water when ready.

Brown rice flour-is the main flour in our Free State flour blends, brown rice flour is gluten-free and contains more fiber and nutrition than white rice flour, though they can be used interchangeably. I prefer to use brown rice flour supplied by Ener-G to eliminate cross-contamination concerns. **www.ener-g.com**

Canola oil- a flavorless oil which makes it ideal for baking. Read carefully for oils that claim to not be cross-contaminated, as it is very easy for this to happen in the manufacturing plant. Most cooking oil producers also make peanut and soy oil, so keep this in mind. Crisco offers the safety assurance label. Spectrum bottles several different nut oils, which are not processed on the premises, but since some of their oils share equipment that has been used to process their nut oils, you may need to avoid their oils.

Chocolate- Enjoy Life is my superhero here in providing several varieties of chocolate bars as well as Mega Chunks and mini chocolate chips for baking. I like to add them to pancakes or waffles, even oatmeal! Purchase locally, or consider stocking up at **www.enjoylifefoods.com**

Cocoa powder- One brand that is readily available is Hershey's, which has an allergy-safe statement. Otherwise, any local supplier that has an allergy- safe seal of approval will work.

Coconut- While you may think coconut is a tree nut (I certainly did!) most allergy authorities, such as The American Academy of Allergy, Asthma, and Immunology do not. It is categorized as a drupaceous fruit, like peaches and nectarines, and has shown minimal allergic response. In fact, the majority of those who are allergic to coconut are not allergic to tree nuts and vice versa. I use unsweetened flaked coconut, coconut oil, coconut milk, cream of coconut, and coconut yogurt as a healthful dairy substitute.

Coconut Aminos- this is a highly nutritious and versatile product that I recommend as a substitute for soy sauce and Asian style sauces. Coconut aminos are gluten-free, soy-free, and vegan, and most varieties are also considered "raw" for those who refer to consume as little cooked foods as possible. The brand most readily available is Coconut Secret **www.coconutsecret.com**

Corn- corn flour, corn meal (also called polenta), and cornstarch all meet the gluten-free and common allergen seal of approval. Please look for brands labeled organic and GMO (genetically modified organism) free for the purest product. Ener-G at **www.ener-g.com**

Dried fruit- look for dried fruit that is not prepared with sugar or sulfur for the safest, most healthful option. Most natural grocers and even your local grocery store should have a wide variety of dried fruits, especially raisins and cranberries that meet these criteria.

Egg Replacer- one of the key products that enabled us to gain our baking freedom, Ener-G Egg Replacer, is allergy-friendly and easy to use. This will not make omelets or egg salad, but instead is created to replace the action that eggs have in cooking. I highly recommend this product and would be at a loss without it. Found at most groceries, or order online at **www.ener-g.com**

Flaxseed Meal- high in Omega 3s, flaxseed meal is a super food that when mixed with hot water creates a gel that can replace eggs in some recipes. Keep flax in the refrigerator, as it's volatile oils can go rancid easily. High quality flax seed suppliers include Premium Gold Flax Products **www.flaxpremiumgold.com**

Fruit-the part of a flowering plant that derives from specific tissues of the flower. Fruits are the means by which many plants disseminate seeds. Believed by many ancient cultures as the most spiritual of all foods, fruit is a vital food for all humankind. Please purchase local fruit in season whenever possible, preferably organic.

Fruit Pectin- is produced commercially as a white to light brown powder, mainly extracted from citrus fruits, and is used in food as a gelling agent particularly in jams and jellies, and some gluten-free baking items. Ball® is one brand that is allergy friendly and is certified kosher.

Garbanzo (chickpea) flour- sometimes referred to as besan or chickpea flour, garbanzo flour is high in protein and gluten-free, and is one of the staples in our Free State flour blend #2. Avoid if cross-contamination from nut flours will affect your health. If you choose this flour, I recommend Bob's **www.bobsredmill.com**

Gluten-free oats- a controversial item, oats are gluten-free if grown and processed in strict accordance to the gluten-free practices. Most of us that reacted to oats were actually reacting to cross-contamination. Look for rolled oats and oat flour clearly labeled gluten-free, such as Bob's Red Mill **www.bobsredmill.com** to be safe. However, cross-contamination from nut or soy flour may be a concern with some suppliers, so read carefully and contact the manufacturer if you have any questions.

Leafy Greens- The best food source for the human body is leafy greens. Kale, collards, spinach, chard, mustard greens, turnip greens, and beet greens are available year round. Eaten raw or cooked, you can never go wrong adding more greens to your diet.

Maple Syrup- even those with tree nut allergies typically can use maple syrup, which is a great unrefined natural sweetener. However, if you have been told to avoid maple syrup, feel free to use agave nectar and add a dash of molasses to the mix. Coombs Family farms is a great brand **www.coombsfamilyfarms.com**

Millet- a small, yellow, gluten-free grain with a mild, corn-like flavor, millet is a staple in gluten-free cooking. It is one of the more environmentally friendly crops which help Earth sustainability. Avoid if cross-contamination from nut flours could affect your health unless clearly labeled as safe.

Molasses- a dark, thick, intensely flavored liquid sweetener high in iron. Given its strong flavor, molasses is never used as the main sweetener. I prefer Wholesome Sweeteners **www.wholesomesweeteners.com**

Mushrooms the fleshy, spore-bearing fruiting body of a fungus, mushrooms are a mainstay in vegan cooking. The most popular are white button (agaricus), portabella, shiitake, crimini, and oyster. Mushrooms are a good source of Vitamin D, protein, copper, and manganese.

Noodles- gluten-free noodles are readily available made from rice, corn, quinoa, amaranth, and buckwheat. Please make sure your noodles clearly state they are wheat-free and gluten-free as it is common to see flour blends that are not 100% gluten-free.

Nutritional yeast- a deactivated yeast which is sold commercially as a food product. It's sold in the form of flakes or as a yellow powder similar in texture to cornmeal, and can be found in the bulk aisle of most natural food stores. It is gluten-free, soy-free, and does not contain the strain of yeast responsible for candida yeast infections. It is high in protein, and is often fortified with B12, so it makes an ideal condiment for our dietary needs. You can sprinkle it on popcorn, use instead of parmesan cheese, or on salads for a boost. Its flavor is slightly cheesy and nutty.

Pasta- Like noodles, pasta is available in a wide variety of shapes and sizes with many gluten-free flours. In the last few years, obtaining gluten-free pasta at your local grocer has become very easy, so chances are, you can get gluten-free, egg-free pasta in your hometown.

Potato flour and potato starch-not the same product, but both are gluten-free and useful in baking. Potato starch is a great substitute for arrowroot, cornstarch, or tapioca, and the flour works well in blends for breads and other baked goods. The safest supplier is Ener-G foods **www.ener-g.com**

Quinoa- an ancient South American grain that has more protein than any other grain, so it's a great food source for vegans. Quinoa flakes and flour can be used to replace oat if you are allergic. Avoid if cross-contamination from nut flours could affect your health unless clearly labeled as safe. I like Ancient Harvest Quinoa Corporation at **www.quinoa.net**

Rice- a seed that is the most important staple food for a large part of the world's human population. Many varieties of rice are available, all of which are gluten-free. I recommend using whole rices such as brown rice, red rice, and black rice (sometimes called forbidden rice).

Salad Greens- A wealth of vegetables are especially useful for salads, such as arugula, watercress, chicory, romaine, red and green leaf lettuces, and iceberg, but do not ignore Boston lettuce, bibb, and endive. All boast their own unique flavor and nutrients.

Sea salt- Sea salt has less sodium than its traditional, processed, iodine enriched counterpart. I like true sea salt, Celtic sea salt, and pink Himalayan sea salt, as they all have more nutrition. I like Hain's **www.hainpurefoods.com**

Seeds- Edible seeds that are not in the nut family include chia, sesame, poppy, pumpkin, quinoa, flax, and sunflower. These are great on salads, stirred into rice or hot cooked grains, or blended into a smoothie.

Shortening- I will only use vegetable shortening, and not lard or any animal based shortenings. I find the idea of animal fat in baked goods to be disturbing, to be honest. I highly recommend Spectrum, who has made a statement that their shortening is allergy-friendly and free from nut oil contamination, and is also dairy-free, soy-free, and vegan. Spectrum offers regular and butter flavored. I use both here a lot. Visit Spectrum's web site for more information at **www.spectrumorganics.com**

Sorghum- a protein rich grain which makes a great gluten-free flour. We use sorghum in our Free State blend #2 for those who will not react to the possibly of nut flour contamination. I prefer Bob's sorghum flour **www.bobsredmill.com**

Spices- A spice is a dried seed, fruit, root, bark, or vegetative substance primarily used for flavoring, coloring or preserving food. Many spices have healing properties, such as oregano and turmeric. McCormick boasts a gluten-free statement on their web site, but other suppliers of safe spices are readily available in your local community.

Squashes- come many varieties, and often we break them into two categories- the summer types (most popular are zucchini and yellow squash) and winter variety (spaghetti squash, pumpkin, butternut, acorn, etc.). I use squashes quite frequently, and I suggest you befriend them as well.

Sugar- I highly recommend using raw sugar or another, less refined variety than white sugar in our recipes, though I am aware it can be far more costly. Look for vegan sugar if you can, as many brands of white sugar are processed using animal bones to make it white and super fine. Raw sugar, sometimes called Sucanat or evaporated cane juice crystals, retains much of its nutritional value and is therefore less likely to deplete your teeth and bones in order for your body to metabolize it. We also use brown sugar and confectioner's sugar in many recipes, too, and I recommend organic if possible. Confectioner's is generally processed with cornstarch, but read the label to be sure nothing else has been added. Try Wholesome Sweeteners **www.wholesomesweeteners.com**

Sunflower seeds and butter- Brands such as SunButter have been providing us with peanut and tree nut-free butters for our eating and baking needs for quite some time, and I think they are wonderful. Sunflower seeds are higher in other nutrition, such as calcium, than peanuts, so it's a highly recommended swap even for those who can have peanuts. Visit **www.sunbutter.com**

Tapioca- extracted from the Cassava melon, tapioca is a great gluten-free additive. Use the pearls for a pudding or the starch as a thickener or flour. Some recipes specify quick-cooking, or instant, tapioca, so please know there is a difference. It is not instant unless the package clearly states this. Brands to try- Ener-G foods **www.ener-g.com** and Let's Do Organic **www.edwardsandsons.com**

Vanilla and other extracts- There are many wheat-free, gluten-free varieties available. In doing my research, McCormick makes this statement, but there are many others who are coming onto the market with new labeling. I refer to this as GF (gluten-free) vanilla in the recipes. I like Elana's Pantry **www.elanaspantry.com**

Vegetable stock- a stock is made by simmering various vegetables in water. You can easily make stock yourself, or purchase any brand that is vegan and clearly states gluten-free on the label. I like Imagine Foods **www.imaginefoods.com**

Vegetables- the edible part of a plant, but usually excludes seeds and most sweet fruit. This typically means the leaf, stem, or root of a plant. Vegetable varieties include leafy greens such as spinach, salad greens such as romaine lettuce, root vegetables like beets and carrots, allium vegetables (onions, garlic, shallots), cruciferous (broccoli, cabbage, cauliflower), and squashes.

Xanthan gum/Guar gum- the product by which if we omit it, gluten-free baking will simply not happen. This powder mimics gluten, and a little goes a long way, which offsets the initial purchase cost. Get xanthan at Ener-G foods **www.ener-g.com** If you cannot have corn products, then guar gum is for you, as xanthan is a corn product. However, the reason why I do not feature guar gum is because it is almost always a soy-based product, so please read the label and contact the manufacturer if soy is a problem for you.

Yeast- needed for some of our breakfast goodies, rapid-rise yeast is gluten-free and best for our needs here. Hodgson Mills **www.hodgsonmills.com**

The Perishable Pantry
Recommended Supplies and Suppliers

Coconut milk- as mentioned earlier, most who are allergic to nuts and tree nuts are not allergic to coconut, so coconut milk is a great alternative. I especially like cream of coconut as a cream replacement. I prefer So Delicious, who offers coconut milk in aseptic containers on the shelf, and refrigerated in the dairy case. **www.sodeliciousdairyfree.com**

Flax Milk- Good Karma advertises on their web site that their products are gluten-free, vegan, allergen-free, and soy-free, and I am a fan. For more information, please visit **www.goodkarmafoods.com**

Hemp milk- Overall, hemp milk has the most nutrition of any of the non-dairy, non-soy milks, and even though it may taste nutty, is totally nut-free. Living Harvest is a good supplier that has a allergy-safe message on their web site. **www.livingharvest.com**

Rice milk- the most popular and oldest of the dairy-free, non-soy milk substitutes available, rice milk is made from brown rice and is generally thinner than the other milks due to its lower fat content. Good Karma and other suppliers readily advertise gluten-free, allergen-free facilities, so you may have many local options to choose from.

Earth Balance- this brand has a soy-free vegan buttery spread that is wonderful for topping muffins, and just about anything else, but its high water content may sometimes skew the results in baking. As such I use shortening or coconut oil instead.

Coconut oil- I highly endorse coconut oil that has been refrigerated as a stick butter substitute in most recipes. Refrigerating it yields an almost shortening-like consistency in its texture. Go for any virgin coconut oil brand that is readily available.

Spectrum Shortening- The shortening itself seems to go from a bit too soft to a bit too hard easily since it is lard-free, so I keep mine in the refrigerator and warm it slightly if needed.

Cheese- While other brands are bound to be available in smaller, local exchanges, the most readily available gluten-free, soy-free, vegan cheese is made by the Daiya company. When I crave cheese, I use Daiya, which comes in shreds as well as wedges. Available nationwide. **www.daiyafoods.com**

Yogurt-Recently, there has been an increase in non-dairy yogurts available. Ricera is a brand using rice milk, and So Delicious, among others, are now offering coconut yogurt.

Cooking Tips, Tricks, Tools, and Supplies
Everything you Need to get Cooking

First of all, you simply cannot cook gluten-free, allergy-friendly foods without a few key staples. The first and perhaps most important of these items is gluten-free flour. There are many all-purpose, gluten-free brands available in most grocers, but as each company has their own blend, each will yield a different result. You are certainly welcome to use any that you have grown fond of, but before blends were readily available, I created two of my own.

Why two blends? I call #1 the safest, for those who are very sensitive, and blend #2 for those who are not going to have a reaction from cross-contamination of tree nuts or soy products. Each blend is slightly different in the flours selected, but you can use either blend you wish. Most manufacturers of bean and ancient gluten-free flours also process soy and nut flours, which is my concern for some of you. See pages **** on converting US measurements to metrics for those of you living outside of the US.

Free State Flour Blend #1- safest
4 cups brown rice flour, superfine
1 cup potato starch
1 cup tapioca starch

Free State Flour Blend #2
2 cups brown rice flour, superfine
1 cup sorghum flour
1 cup garbanzo bean flour
1 cup tapioca starch
1 cup arrowroot

For those whose systems are very sensitive, I highly recommend getting all the ingredients offered by Ener-G Foods locally or online for blend #1. They are the only company at time of writing this book who guarantees a dedicated nut and tree nut free facility, in addition to being gluten, egg, dairy, wheat, and soy-free. Others may certainly exist, especially at the local level, but as I have been in this field for over 16 years, this is the company I started with, and will continue to rely on for my most sensitive eaters.

Superfine flour really helps take away some of the grit you may experience in baking. While there are some suppliers advertising their flour is superfine, I have been baking this way long before such a variety was available, so I use a coffee grinder or blender to process my rice flour in small batches to help make it even smoother. You do not need to do this, but I have found it really does improve the results.

Otherwise, baking with either blend is no different than using regular flour. Just like traditional flour, when you need to measure it, use a dry measuring cup, level it with a flat surface like a butter knife, and make sure the cup is full without overflowing.

From experience, I have learned that these flours are a bit more delicate however, so instead of scooping it out of your container with the actual measuring cup, use a large spoon. These flours have a higher tendency of packing, and while firmly packed is usually recommended for brown sugar, firmly packed flour usually yields poor results in a cookie recipe.

So, after you have processed your rice flour and obtained a large airtight container, spoon out each of these flours into a dry measuring cup, put a large container or bowl, and gently stir to incorporate. Keep stored in the refrigerator for best results. Do not add any baking soda, baking powder, or xanthan gum to this blend, as they can lose their potency quickly.

Kitchen Tools

Some of these are more vital to your dessert making than others, but here is what I recommend to have on hand in your kitchen.

Blender
Bowls in assorted sizes
Cake stand/storage container to preserve freshness
Coffee grinder for superfine flours and making your own flaxseed meal
Cookie and biscuit cutters
Cutting board
Decorating supplies and items- frosting bags, sprinkles, etc.
Electric mixer- stand up or hand held
Flour sifter
Food processor
Kitchen timer
Knives
Measuring tools- liquid cups, dry cups, and spoons
Microplane/zester
Muffin paper liners
Oven mitts/pot holders
Packaging items- plastic wrap, aluminum foil, baggies, etc.
Parchment paper
Pastry blender
Pastry cutter for lattice pie making
Pots and pans of various sizes
Rolling pin
Skillets
Toothpicks
Utensils- wooden spoons, serving utensils, spatulas, whisks, etc.
Vegetable peeler
Wire cooling rack
Wok

Breakfasts

Called the most important meal of the day, breakfast helps you wake up and get your engine going.

Whether you prefer a light snack or a hearty, filling meal, our selection is sure to satisfy everyone at your table with an assortment of morning options from around the world.

Bagels

Makes 1 dozen

Bagels are a traditional breakfast item, especially in the Northeast, just as biscuits are common in the South and Midwest regions.

○○

3 cups Free State flour, page 11
2 teaspoons flaxseed meal
1 Tablespoon xanthan gum
2 Tablespoons agave nectar
1 teaspoon apple cider vinegar
1 teaspoon granulated sweetener
Cornmeal for dusting pan
1½ teaspoons Egg Replacer

1 teaspoon sea salt
1¼ cups warm water
1 Tablespoon dry yeast
2 Tablespoons canola oil
1¼ cups warm water
Flour for dusting surface
Seeds or other toppings

Line a cookie sheet with parchment paper and sprinkle with cornmeal. Set aside.

Grease and flour a second cookie sheet. Set aside.

Place flour, sea salt, flax meal, Egg Replacer, xanthan gum, and yeast into a mixing bowl and whisk together with a wooden spoon.

In a separate bowl, whisk together agave nectar, oil, vinegar, and warm water. Using an electric mixer, slowly incorporate the liquid mixture into dry ingredients. Add more warm water, if necessary, to create smooth consistency. Beat on medium-high speed for 3 minutes. Mixture may be quite thick and sticky.

Lightly roll dough in the dusting flour and roll into 12 balls of equal size. Flatten each bagel slightly and poke a hole in the center of each. Place each bagel on the cookie sheet sprinkled with cornmeal. Allow bagels to rise, about 30 minutes.

Once bagels have risen, bring a large stockpot of water to boil.

Preheat oven to 375°F.

Drop a few bagels into the boiling water. Simmer for 30 seconds, turn over, and boil for another 30 seconds. Using a slotted spoon, remove bagels, draining as much excess water as possible. If you are adding toppings, such as sesame seeds, dredge each bagel, one at a time, in a bowl of the chosen topping, and shake off excess. Place bagels on the floured cookie sheet.

Once all bagels are boiled/topped, bake for 25 minutes. Cool on a wire rack for 5 minutes before serving. You can serve with Earth Balance soy-free spread or the jam or jelly of your choice.

Chocolate Chip Pancakes

Serves 4

Pancakes were one of my favorite breakfasts as a child, so it was important for me to create something healthy, safe, and still delicious for the kitchen.

¾ cup buckwheat flour
1½ cups vanilla coconut milk
¼ cup applesauce
1 Tablespoon Egg Replacer
1 Tablespoon gluten-free vanilla
2 Tablespoons agave nectar
½ teaspoon sea salt
Coconut oil for greasing skillet

½ cup gluten-free oat flour
2 Tablespoons canola oil
2 teaspoons baking powder
¼ cup water
1 cup Enjoy Life Mini chips
2 Tablespoons raw sugar
½ teaspoon cinnamon

Prepare Egg Replacer with water. Stir well and set aside.

In a large bowl, combine all the dry ingredients, except chocolate chips. Stir with a wooden spoon. Whisk in the applesauce and prepared Egg Replacer until well combined. Add vanilla, coconut milk, canola oil, and agave nectar, and beat with an electric mixer for one minute, until mixture is foamy.

Gently fold in chocolate chips.

Heat a skillet or pancake griddle over medium-high heat. Add enough coconut oil to coat pan.

Test the skillet's temperature by placing a small drop of pancake batter onto the pan. If it begins to sizzle and bubble, the surface is ready.

Pour out about ¼ cup of batter per pancake, and allow for 1 inch of space in between pancakes. Cook until the surface begins to bubble, then gently flip with a pancake spatula. Cook for another 2-3 minutes, until pancakes turn golden. Repeat with remaining batter.

Outrageous Oatmeal

Serves 2

When you discover you cannot have something as simple and basic as oatmeal, you begin to miss it. Now with the advent of gluten-free oats, you likely can have them again. Of the many ways you can prepare oatmeal, I prefer this hearty method.

○○

1 cup gluten-free old fashioned rolled oats
1 medium banana, sliced
1 Tablespoon sunflower seed butter
2 Tablespoons raw sugar
2 Tablespoons shredded coconut

1¼ cups vanilla rice milk
2 Tablespoons maple syrup
¼ teaspoon sea salt
¼ teaspoon cinnamon

In a small saucepan, combine oats, milk, sea salt, and cinnamon. Bring to almost boiling, then reduce heat and simmer, stirring frequently for 3-5 minutes, until creamy.

Remove from heat. Stir in sunflower seed butter, maple syrup, and banana. Top with raw sugar and coconut just before serving.

Other Options

Instead of the above variety, cook the oatmeal in rice milk and add any of the following:

¼ cup each dried raisins, cranberries, and blueberries
1 Tablespoon pumpkin seeds and 1 teaspoon flax seeds
2 Tablespoons jam of choice and ½ cup fruit
¼ cup dried apples and stir in 2 Tablespoons applesauce

Biscuits and Gravy

Makes 12 biscuits, Serves 4

Biscuits and gravy are a popular breakfast combination in the Southern and Midwestern states, so I could not ignore the need to invent a Free State version for those of you who would be lost without them.

ooooooooooooooooooooooooooooooooooooooooooooooooooooooooooooooooooooooooooooooooooooooooooooooooo

Biscuits

1½ cups Free State flour, page 11
2 Tablespoons double acting baking powder
½ cup Spectrum butter flavored shortening
½ teaspoon xanthan gum

2 Tablespoons raw sugar
½ teaspoon sea salt
½ cup plain coconut milk

White Gravy

2 Tablespoons tapioca starch
5 Tablespoons Earth Balance soy-free spread
¼ teaspoon black pepper

1 cup plain rice milk
½ teaspoon sea salt

Preheat oven to 375°F. Grease a cookie sheet with coconut oil or shortening. Set aside.

Combine the flour, raw sugar, baking powder, xanthan gum, and sea salt in a large bowl. Using a fork or pastry blender, cut in the shortening until dough is crumbly. Stir in milk and form a ball.

Flour a countertop or large cutting board and turn dough out onto the surface. Flour your hands and a rolling pin, and knead dough until it loses its stickiness. Roll out until the dough is ½ inch thick.

Using a biscuit cutter or wide mouthed glass, cut out 12 equal sized biscuits and place on the cookie sheet.

Bake on the center rack of the oven for 10-12 minutes, or until the tops begin to yield a light golden hue. While the biscuits are baking, prepare the white gravy.

Heat a small saucepan over medium heat. Add the Earth Balance and melt. Stir in tapioca starch and milk and whisk vigorously to create a thick ragout. Add sea salt and pepper, then bring to quick boil, stirring continuously. Reduce heat to low, and continue stirring until it begins to thicken. Turn off heat and let stand until the biscuits are ready.

If the sauce appears too thick for your preference, add more milk. If it is too thin, you can blend a bit more tapioca starch in a small amount of cold water, then add to the gravy.

Serve three biscuits, split, with gravy on both pieces.

Groovy Gluten-Free Granola

Makes 10 servings, ½ cup each

Great with fruit, non-dairy, soy-free yogurt, or just for snacking.

1 cup gluten-free puffed rice cereal
½ cup pumpkin seeds
½ cup pitted dates, chopped
½ cup sesame seeds
½ Tablespoon flax meal
1 teaspoon cinnamon
1 Tablespoon gluten-free oat flour

1 cup gluten-free rolled oats
½ cup sunflower seeds
½ cup shredded coconut
½ cup dried blueberries
¼ cup maple syrup
2 Tablespoons raw sugar
¼ cup coconut oil, in pieces

Preheat oven to 325°F. Grease a cookie sheet with coconut oil and set aside.

Combine all ingredients, and dot with pieces of coconut oil on top.

Spread on cookie sheet. Bake uncovered on center rack of the oven for 40 minutes, rotating pan after 20 minutes.

Allow to cool 10 minutes before removing from cookie sheet.

Transfer to a glass or heat safe storage container and allow to finish the cooling process in this container.

Granola will stay fresh for up to two weeks at room temperature.

Morning Stew

Serves 4

You can make this with whatever available fruit or seeds you have on hand, but this is my favorite combination.

°°°

2 cups cooked rice or other gluten-free grain
1 medium ripe banana, sliced
½ cup sliced strawberries
1 large apple, chopped
¼ cup sunflower seeds
2 Tablespoons rice syrup

2 cups plain rice milk
½ cup blueberries
½ cup pineapple tidbits, drained
½ teaspoon cinnamon
¼ cup shredded coconut
¼ cup sesame seeds

Heat milk in a medium saucepan. Add cinnamon, rice syrup, coconut, and apple. Simmer until just boiling, about 3 minutes.

Reduce heat and stir in your rice/grain. Simmer and stir frequently until heated through and creamy, about 3-5 minutes.

Serve by scooping grain equally into 4 bowls, then top with berries, banana, and seeds. Top with additional rice syrup, if desired.

Start of the Day Casserole

Serves 4

Sometimes I wake up really hungry and need a filling meal, and this casserole really does the trick for me. If I am extra hungry, I serve with gluten-free toast or bread from our bread selection starting on page 51.

ooooooooooooooooooooooooooooooooooooooooooooooooooooooooooooooooooooooooooooo

1 pound small red potatoes, quartered
1 medium yellow onion, chopped
1 cup sliced button mushrooms
2 Tablespoons nutritional yeast
1 teaspoon black pepper
1 teaspoon dried oregano
2 Tablespoons olive oil
¼ cup vegetable stock

1 medium green pepper, diced
1 cup fresh spinach leaves
1 medium red bell pepper, diced
1 teaspoon sea salt
1 teaspoon paprika
2 large tomatoes, diced
1 teaspoon curry powder

Preheat oven to 400°F. Grease a 9x13 baking pan with coconut oil. Set aside.

In a large skillet, sauté onions, peppers, mushrooms, and potatoes in vegetable stock for 10 minutes over medium heat, stirring frequently. You may need to add more stock to prevent mixture from sticking.

Stir in tomato and all spices, then transfer to baking pan. Top with olive oil.

Roast on the center rack of the oven uncovered for 15 minutes, rotate pan, and bake another 10 minutes or until potatoes are cooked and slightly crispy.

Aloo Puha

Serves 4

While you may not yet be adventurous enough to swap your morning oatmeal for spicy Indian rice dish, I really suggest you try. Spices wake up the metabolism and the nutrients from cooked grains, especially when vegetables are added, sustain you until lunch. It is also a great way to reuse leftovers.

2 cups cooked rice, any variety
1 large yellow onion, chopped coarsely
¼ cup cooked lentils
½ cup spinach or any other leafy greens
4 Tablespoons melted coconut oil
Juice of 1 lemon

1 large potato, cubed and peeled
2 green chilies, seeded and chopped
¼ teaspoon mustard seeds
1 pinch curry powder
1 pinch turmeric powder
Sea salt and pepper, to taste

Soak the cooked rice in water for at least 30 minutes, or overnight. Rinse and drain, then stir in 1 tablespoon melted coconut oil, sea salt, turmeric powder, and curry, and set aside.

Peel and cut the potato into small cubes. Chop the onions and chilies into desired size pieces. Set aside,

Heat remaining coconut oil and place lentils, mustard seeds, and greens into a large frying pan over medium heat. Cook and stir frequently until the seeds begin to pop and sizzle.

Add potatoes, onion, and chilies, and cook till the potatoes are soft, approximately 20 minutes.

Add rice and reduce heat. Stir frequently to prevent sticking. Cook for 5-7 minutes, or until rice is hot. Remove from heat and add lemon juice just before serving.

Can't Taste the Zucchini Bread

Makes one 7x4x3 loaf- 8 slices

The first time I heard about zucchini bread was at a friend's house hosting a women's healing circle. I was unable to try it because of my allergies, but everyone said it was delicious and did not taste like zucchini. Here is the Free State version, which I hear is just as good, if not better, than the original. A big thank you to Lisa for the inspiration.

1½ cups Free State flour, page 11
½ teaspoon baking soda
1 teaspoon baking powder
½ teaspoon sea salt
1 cup raw grated zucchini
½ cup mashed banana
¾ teaspoon xanthan gum

¼ cup melted coconut oil
¾ cup raw sugar
¼ cup flaxseed meal
1 Tablespoon gluten-free vanilla
½ cup golden raisins
½ cup Enjoy Life Mini chips
¼ cup gluten-free rolled oats

Preheat oven to 350°F. Grease a 7x4x3 loaf pan with coconut oil and set aside.

In a medium bowl, combine flour, baking soda, baking powder, sea salt, xanthan gum, and flaxseed. Stir with a wooden spoon and set aside.

Combine mashed banana, melted coconut oil, raw sugar, vanilla, raisins, and grated zucchini. Mix well, then stir in the dry ingredients. Fold in the mini chips.

Transfer batter to the greased pan and sprinkle with gluten-free rolled oats.

Bake on the center rack of the oven for 30 minutes, rotate pan, and continue to bake another 30-40 minutes, until the top is golden and a toothpick comes out clean.

Allow pan to cool on a wire rack for 15 minutes before removing loaf from pan.

Doughnuts
Makes 1 dozen

Just when you had probably gotten over your habit of doughnuts and coffee, here is a recipe to bring that all back. This recipe is lower in fat because I use a mini doughnut pan to bake instead of fry them. I love these with chocolate coconut milk.

1 cup Free State flour, page 11
½ cup raw sugar
¼ teaspoon sea salt
1 teaspoon gluten-free vanilla extract
½ teaspoon xanthan gum
1½ teaspoons Egg Replacer

¼ cup cocoa powder
1 teaspoon baking powder
½ cup chocolate coconut milk
¼ cup coconut oil
1 teaspoon baking soda
2 Tablespoons water

Preheat oven to 350°F. Grease doughnut pan with coconut oil and set aside.

Prepare Egg Replacer with water. Stir well and set aside.

In a large bowl, combine all dry ingredients and mix thoroughly. Add prepared Egg Replacer and stir well.

Combine coconut oil, vanilla, and coconut milk in a small sauce pan over medium low heat and heat until the coconut oil is melted. Add to dry ingredients and mix until just combined.

Spoon batter into each doughnut well until 2/3 of the way full.

Bake for 6 minutes, rotate pan, and bake another 6 minutes, or until a toothpick comes out clean.

Allow to cool completely before removing from pan.

Country Breakfast

Makes 4 Servings

I was never a fan of cold cereal or cold breakfasts, even as a child, so this big country breakfast really works for me. You'll never miss the eggs or meat.

ooooooooooooooooooooooooooooooooooooooooooooooooooooooooooooooooooooooooooooooooo

Cheese Grits

¾ cup dry grits
1 cup Daiya shredded cheddar cheese
2 Tablespoons Earth Balance soy-free spread

3 cups water
Pinch of sea salt
Pinch of black pepper

Preheat oven to 350°F.

Bring water to a boil and stir in grits and cook according to package directions.

After it has cooked, pour into a 1½ quart greased casserole dish. Mix in the Earth Balance and cheese, stirring constantly until thoroughly mixed.

Bake uncovered for 30 minutes or until top is set and lightly puffy. Let stand 5 minutes before serving.

While this is making, prepare the fried apples.

Fried Apples

5 large apples, peeled, cored, and sliced
¼ cup maple syrup
A pinch sea salt
¼ teaspoon ginger

¼ cup coconut oil
1 teaspoon cinnamon
2 Tablespoons raw sugar
¼ teaspoon nutmeg

Melt coconut oil in a medium-sized pan over medium heat. Add apples, ginger, sea salt, sugar, cinnamon, and nutmeg, and cook slowly, turning slices as they start to brown. When they are soft on both sides, add the syrup. Simmer on the stovetop for 15 minutes.

Top with our granola, page 19, for additional crunch.

Waffles

Makes 4 Servings

Most of my recipes were created out of necessity, before it was possible to find gluten-free, vegan, and nut-free waffles in the freezer section of a natural food store. I like to use the leftovers for waffles and ice cream later.

°°

2 cups Free State flour, page 11
1½ cups plain unsweetened rice milk
1 teaspoon xanthan gum
1 Tablespoon Egg Replacer
2 Tablespoons agave nectar
¼ cup water

½ teaspoon sea salt
3 teaspoons baking powder
4 Tablespoons melted coconut oil
¼ teaspoon cinnamon
Maple Syrup and other toppings

In a small bowl, prepare Egg Replacer with water. Stir well and set aside.

In a separate bowl, combine all dry ingredients. Add rice milk, melted coconut oil, prepared Egg Replacer, and agave nectar. Mix with an electric mixer for 30 seconds.

Grease your waffle iron and preheat. Test batter by placing a small drop on the waffle iron. If it begins to sizzle, the waffle iron is ready.

Pour a ladle of batter onto the waffle iron and cook until the waffle is done, generally 3-5 minutes for most standard models.

Repeat until all batter is used. Top with Earth Balance soy-free spread and syrup, or with your favorite toppings.

Fig Compote

When my sweet tooth kicks in but I want to stay with something on the healthy side, I like to serve this with my Heavenly Graham Crackers from my other book *Free State Bakery's Nothing to Sneeze At,* or any of Enjoy Life's cookies.

1 cup apple cider
½ teaspoon molasses
1 Tablespoon fresh lemon juice
½ cup dried figs, sliced
½ teaspoon ground ginger
1 teaspoon gluten-free vanilla extract

¼ cup raw sugar
¼ cup water
½ cup dried apricots, quartered
½ cup dried cranberries
¼ teaspoon cinnamon

Simmer apple cider, sugar, molasses, water, and lemon juice in a medium saucepan, stirring occasionally until molasses and sugar are dissolved.

Add fruit and seasonings. Simmer 5 minutes, or until the fruits are plump and liquid is slightly thick. Allow to cool completely.

Refrigerate for at least one hour before serving. Serve chilled.

Carrot Bread

Makes one 9x5x3 loaf, 8 slices

Not quite a muffin, but certainly not a cake, this loaf is not too sweet and is loaded with vitamins to start your day off right.

○○○

1½ cups Free State flour, page 11
1 Tablespoon Egg Replacer
¼ cup applesauce
1 teaspoon baking soda
1 teaspoon xanthan gum
1 cup shredded carrots
1 teaspoon cinnamon

¾ cup agave nectar
¼ cup pineapple juice
2 teaspoons baking powder
½ teaspoon sea salt
½ cup raisins
¼ cup pineapple tidbits
½ cup melted coconut oil

Preheat oven to 350°F. Grease loaf pan with coconut oil and set aside.

Prepare Egg Replacer with pineapple juice in a large bowl. Add melted coconut oil and agave nectar, and stir with a wooden spoon. Whisk in applesauce, raisins, and all dry ingredients. Beat with an electric mixer for 1 minute.

Fold in carrots and pineapple carefully.

Pour into pan. Bake on the center rack of the oven for 30 minutes, rotate pan, and continue to bake another 15-20 minutes, until a toothpick comes out clean.

Transfer pan to a wire rack and cool for 30 minutes before removing and slicing.

Blueberry Coffee Cake

Makes one 9x9 pan, 8-12 servings

This is a delicious cake for those who have to have something sweet in the morning.

Cake

2 cups Free State flour, page 11
1 teaspoon double-acting baking powder
1 cup plain coconut yogurt
1 cup raw sugar
½ cup cold coconut oil
1 Tablespoon Egg Replacer
1 cup fresh blueberries

½ teaspoon xanthan gum
1 teaspoon sea salt
1 teaspoon baking soda
1 teaspoon GF vanilla
1 teaspoon cider vinegar
¼ cup coconut milk
2 Tablespoons blueberry jam

Crumb Topping

1½ cups Free State flour, page 11
½ cup Spectrum butter shortening
1 cup packed dark brown sugar
2 Tablespoons confectioner's sugar

½ teaspoon xanthan gum
½ teaspoon sea salt
1 teaspoon cinnamon

Preheat oven to 325°F. Grease and flour a 9x9 baking pan.

Prepare Egg Replacer with coconut milk. Set aside.

Combine coconut yogurt and cider vinegar in a small bowl. Set aside.

Create the cake ingredients by combining the flour, gum, baking powder, soda, and sea salt. Stir well. Cut in the cold coconut oil to make a crumbly mix. Add the raw sugar, prepared Egg Replacer, and vanilla. Beat with an electric mixer for 2-3 minutes, or until the coconut oil is broken down and the batter is smooth. Stir in the yogurt blend and blueberry jam and mix until well incorporated. Transfer batter to the pan. Set aside.

Gently fold in the blueberries.

Prepare the crumb topping by combining the flour, gum, and sea salt. Stir well. Add brown sugar and cinnamon. Cut in the shortening using a fork or pastry blender until the mix turns into small crumbs.

Bake on the center rack for 15 minutes, then remove pan and sprinkle the crumb topping over the cake. Return to the oven, and continue to bake for another 30 minutes, or until a toothpick comes out clean.

Allow to cool for 15 minutes before sprinkling confectioner's sugar on top.

Corn Muffins

Makes 1 dozen

I have fond memories of going to a small diner as a child and having a toasted corn muffin with chocolate milk as a summer breakfast, and these muffins taste just as good.

2½ cups Free State flour, page 11
½ cup Spectrum butter shortening
¾ teaspoon xanthan gum
1½ teaspoons double acting baking powder
1 cup rice milk
1 Tablespoon Egg Replacer
2 teaspoons gluten-free vanilla

¾ cup cornmeal
1 Tablespoon lemon juice
1½ teaspoons baking soda
1 cup raw sugar
1 teaspoon sea salt
1 cup plain coconut yogurt

Preheat oven to 350°F. Line a muffin pan with 12 paper liners.

Prepare Egg Replacer in a cup by using ¼ cup of rice milk. Set aside.

In a medium sized bowl, combine remaining milk, yogurt, and lemon juice to make a mock buttermilk, and set aside.

In a large bowl, add raw sugar, shortening, and prepared Egg Replacer. Mix with an electric mixer for 30 seconds and set aside.

In a separate bowl, combine the flour, cornmeal, gum, baking powder, baking soda, and sea salt. Stir well. Add dry ingredients to the wet ingredients. Use the electric mixer and mix for 30 seconds, until the dry ingredients are well moistened.

Evenly divide the batter amongst the 12 cups. Bake on the center rack for 15 minutes, rotate pan, and continue to bake another 15 minutes, or until the tops are golden and a toothpick comes out clean.

Cool on a wire rack for 5 minutes before serving.

Cranberry Oat Scones

Makes 1 dozen

My love of scones developed at about the same time as my love of tea, so I find myself often having one of these with a cup of chai.

ooooooooooooooooooooooooooooooooooooooooooooooooooooooooooooooooooooooooooooooooo

2½ cups Free State flour, page 11
¾ teaspoon xanthan gum
½ cup raw sugar
1/3 cup melted coconut oil
2 Tablespoons double-acting baking powder
1 cup fresh cranberries

½ cup gluten-free oat flour
1 Tablespoon lemon juice
1 cup plain coconut yogurt
¾ cup rice milk
½ teaspoon sea salt

Preheat oven to 400°F. Line a cookie sheet with parchment paper.

Combine yogurt, milk, and lemon juice to make a buttermilk substitute. Set aside.

In a separate bowl, combine the flours, gum, raw sugar, baking powder, and sea salt. Stir to combine. Mix in the melted coconut oil and buttermilk, and stir by hand until it forms a lumpy, thick, sticky dough.

Flour a countertop or cutting board as well as your hands, and knead dough until it slightly toughens and loses some of its stickiness. Roll out dough to about ½ inch thickness.

Place cranberries on the right side of the dough, and fold left side of dough over them, enveloping the berries.

Cut your dough in half with a sharp knife. Press each one into a circle, about 5-6 inches in diameter. Cut each into 6 pie wedges, 12 in all, and place each slice on your cookie sheet.

Bake on the center rack of the oven for 15-20 minutes, or until golden and slightly crispy.

Serve warm.

Appetizers

These meal starters are great as the main course when you want a light meal, or when you want a heavy snack.

We took the ones we missed most and reinvented them, so your favorites are bound to be here.

Zucchini Sticks

Makes 4 Servings

Zucchini is a delicious vegetable and is very versatile, so I use it regularly in the warmer months. I like to serve these instead of French fries with a burger.

2 quarts canola oil for frying
2 Tablespoons Egg Replacer
¼ cup plain coconut milk
½ teaspoon black pepper
¼ teaspoon sea salt
¾ cup gluten-free bread crumbs
1 teaspoon dried basil

¼ cup plain coconut milk
½ teaspoon garlic powder
¼ teaspoon sea salt
1 cup Free State flour, page 11
3 medium zucchini, quartered
1 teaspoon oregano
½ teaspoon onion powder

In a heavy skillet or deep fryer, preheat oil to 350°F.

In a blender, add the Egg Replacer, milk, pepper and sea salt. Transfer the mixture to a medium bowl and set aside.

Place your flour in a medium bowl and set aside.

Prepare the breadcrumbs by adding to a medium bowl. Add garlic powder, onion powder, oregano, and basil, and stir to blend.

Slice the zucchini into pieces 2 to 3 inches long. Dip the pieces into the flour, then the egg mixture, and then coat them with the bread crumbs.

Test the oil before frying by adding a drop of water to the oil. If it immediately spits and pops, it is ready for use. Carefully place a few of the battered pieces in the oil and fry 3 to 4 minutes, until brown and crispy. Do not cook too many, or you will reduce the oil's temperature, and potentially affect the results.

Drain on a paper towel. Repeat until all the slices have been fried.

Serve with your favorite marinara sauce, or as a side dish with a burger or sandwich.

Southwestern Egg Rolls

Makes 2 Servings

One of my husband's favorite appetizers, minus the chicken and unsafe ingredients.

2 Tablespoons melted coconut oil
1 portabella mushroom cap, sliced thin
2 Tablespoons minced green onion
2 Tablespoons minced red bell pepper
¼ cup black beans, rinsed and drained
2 Tablespoons chopped spinach leaves
2 Tablespoons diced jalapeno pepper
¾ cup shredded Daiya pepper jack cheese
4 (6 inch) gluten free tortillas

¼ cup frozen corn kernels
½ teaspoon ground cumin
½ teaspoon sea salt
½ teaspoon chili powder
1 quart oil for deep frying
½ Tablespoon dried parsley
1 pinch cayenne pepper

Add coconut oil and sliced portabella mushrooms to a medium skillet. Cook over medium heat, stirring frequently, until the mushrooms begin to wither. Stir in green onion and red peppers. Cook 5 minutes, until tender. Mix in corn, black beans, spinach, jalapeno peppers, parsley, cumin, chili powder, sea salt and cayenne pepper. Cook 5 minutes, remove from heat, and stir in pepper jack cheese.

Wrap tortillas with a clean, lightly moist cloth. Microwave on high approximately 1 minute, or until pliable.

Spoon equal amounts of the mixture into each tortilla. Fold ends of tortillas, then roll tightly around mixture. Secure with toothpicks. Arrange in a medium dish, cover with plastic, and place in the freezer. Freeze at least 4 hours.

When ready to prepare, heat oil in a large, deep skillet or deep fryer to 375°F. Test oil by adding a drop of water to the oil. If it immediately spits and pops, it is ready.

Remove toothpicks, and deep fry 2 tortillas at a time, 10 minutes each, or until dark golden brown.

Drain on paper towels before serving. Repeat until all are cooked. If desired, serve with guacamole and salsa, page 49.

Stuffed Tomatoes

Makes 4 Servings

I like these as a lunch with kale salad in the warmer months.

½ cup dry grits
¾ teaspoon sea salt
1 cup Daiya havarti cheese wedge, diced
¼ cup nutritional yeast
½ cup shredded Daiya mozzarella cheese
1 Tablespoon Egg Replacer
¼ teaspoon crushed red pepper

1½ cups water
8 large tomatoes
1 teaspoon sea salt
2½ teaspoons garlic powder
¼ cup chopped fresh parsley
¼ cup water
½ teaspoon oregano

In a small saucepan combine dry grits, 1½ cups water, and ¾ teaspoon of sea salt. Bring to a boil, then simmer until grits are tender, 15 to 20 minutes, or according to package instructions. Remove from heat and set aside.

Preheat oven to 350°F. Coat a baking sheet with coconut oil. Set aside.

Prepare the Egg Replacer with ¼ cup water in a medium bowl. Mix well, then stir into the cooled grits the havarti cheese cubes, mozzarella, and nutritional yeast. Stir in the garlic powder, parsley, crushed red pepper, and sea salt. Mix well to help the cheeses melt.

Slice the top off of each tomato. Use a spoon to hollow out the tomatoes, leaving the outer shells, approximately ¼ inch thick intact. Fill each with the grits mixture. Arrange stuffed tomatoes on prepared baking sheet.

Bake until light golden brown, 30 to 40 minutes.

Allow to cool slightly before serving.

Corn and Vegetable Fritters

Makes 4 Servings

You can vary which veggies you add, but this is my favorite blend.

2 cups Free State flour, page 11
½ teaspoon cumin
½ teaspoon sea salt
1 Tablespoon Egg Replacer
1 cup plain rice milk
2 cups grated zucchini
¼ cup diced green bell pepper
1 cup shredded Daiya cheddar cheese
¼ cup Earth Balance soy-free spread, melted

1 Tablespoon baking powder
½ cup raw sugar
Fresh ground black pepper
¼ cup water
2 cups grated zucchini
1½ cups fresh corn
¼ cup diced red bell pepper
Oil for frying

Prepare Egg Replacer with ¼ cup of water. Stir well and set aside.

In a large bowl, stir together the flour, baking powder, cumin, sugar, sea salt, and pepper. Set aside.

Add milk, melted Earth Balance, and prepared Egg Replacer into the dry ingredients. Stir in zucchini, corn, peppers, and cheese; mix well.

Heat oil in a heavy skillet over medium-high heat. Check temperature by dropping a small amount of batter into the oil. If it immediately begins to sizzle, the oil is ready. Drop batter, two tablespoons at a time, into hot oil. Fry until crisp and brown, turning once with tongs.

Drain on paper towels and serve immediately.

Thai Spring Rolls

Makes 3 Servings

This is perhaps my favorite appetizer because they are healthy, can be easily modified, and is light enough for warmer days. I will often have 3 with dipping sauce as a meal. Make sure the brand of rice paper wrappers are gluten-free by getting Thai or Vietnamese varieties made with rice flour and tapioca. Traditional Asian wrappers are almost always made with wheat.

Spring Rolls

6 rice paper Spring roll wrappers
¼ cup chopped cilantro
1 medium carrot, julienned

1 cup shredded iceberg lettuce
1 cup cooked sushi rice
1 green onion, sliced fine

Dipping Sauce

1 Tablespoon coconut aminos
1 Tablespoon green onions

1 Tablespoon rice vinegar
A pinch of red pepper flakes, optional

Cook sushi rice according to package instructions, generally ½ cup uncooked rice to 1½ cups water simmered until sticky and soft. Set aside.

Chop all vegetables and place on a plate for assembly convenience.

In a bowl of cool water, soak one wrapper until limp. Lay wrapper out on a flat on a plate. Spread a thin layer of rice, then place 1/6 of the lettuce then other ingredients on top. Fold over each end and tightly roll the wrapper around the contents, as if making a burrito. Moisten at seam and press to close.

Repeat process until all wrappers are made.

To make the dipping sauce, combine all ingredients in a small bowl and whisk together.

Scallion Pancakes

Makes 4 Servings

If you have never had these before at a Chinese restaurant, you are in for a treat. These can best be described as a cross between a potato pancake and pita, as they have a slightly gummy texture but loaded with savory onion flavor.

°°

¼ teaspoon sea salt
1 cup Free State flour, page 11
½ cup finely chopped green onion
2 Tablespoons melted coconut oil
2 Tablespoons coconut oil

¼ cup warm water, more as needed
½ teaspoon xanthan gum
¼ teaspoon canola oil, as needed
Extra flour for your countertop
Coconut aminos, for dipping

Dissolve sea salt in warm water, and mix in 1 cup of flour to make a soft dough. Turn the dough out onto a well-floured work surface, and knead until slightly springy, about 5 minutes. If the dough is sticky, knead in ¼ teaspoon of canola oil.

Divide the dough into 8 equal-size pieces.

On a floured work surface, roll a piece of dough out into a thin square about 5x7 inches in size, brush the dough with melted coconut oil, and sprinkle about 1 tablespoon of chopped green onion onto the dough. Spread the onion out evenly.

Starting with a long end, roll the dough up into a rope shape, and pinch the seam and the ends closed. Roll the rope shape into a flat spiral, and press lightly with your hands to compact the spiral and keep it from unrolling.

Place the spiral down onto the floured work surface, and gently roll it out into a pancake with the onions folded inside, turning the pancake over often as you roll it out. Roll gently and turn often to avoid making holes in the pancake. Finished pancake should be about 5 inches in diameter. Repeat with the rest of the dough pieces, making 8 pancakes total.

Heat a heavy skillet over medium heat, and add 2 Tablespoons coconut oil. Once the oil has melted, pan-fry each pancake until golden brown on both sides, about 5 minutes per side. Cut into wedges and serve warm with coconut aminos or your favorite allergy-friendly dipping sauces.

Jalapeno Poppers
Makes 4 Servings

This is one recipe I had trouble remaking until recently, when Daiya released their "wedge" cheeses. These wedges are softer than hard blocks of cheese, and are easily softened with a fork or spoon to create a cream cheese like, spreadable product.

ooooooooooooooooooooooooooooooooooooooooooooooooooooooooooooooooooooooooooooooooooooooooooo

1 package Daiya pepperjack wedge, softened
1 (8 ounce) package Daiya shredded cheddar cheese
12 jalapeno peppers, seeded and halved
1 cup gluten-free bread crumbs

1 cup plain rice milk
1 cup Free State flour, page 11
2 quarts oil for frying

Cut and halve the jalapenos, using clothes, and remove seeds. Set aside.

In a medium bowl, mix the softened Daiya cheese and shredded cheddar cheese. Spoon this mixture into the jalapeno pepper halves.

Put the milk and flour into two separate small bowls. Dip the stuffed jalapenos first into the milk then into the flour, making sure they are well coated with each. Allow the coated jalapenos to dry for about 10 minutes.

Dip the jalapenos in milk again and roll them through the breadcrumbs. Allow them to dry, then repeat to ensure the entire surface of the jalapeno is coated.

In a medium skillet, heat the oil to 365°F. Deep fry the jalapenos 2 to 3 minutes each, until golden brown. Remove and let drain on a paper towel before serving.

Stuffed Mushrooms

Makes 4 Servings

You can also serve these as sandwiches on one of our gluten-free breads starting on page 51.

4 large portobella mushroom caps
1 Tablespoon balsamic or red wine vinegar
2 Tablespoons water
1 (10 ounce) bag fresh spinach, chopped
3 Tablespoons seasoned gluten-free bread crumbs, divided
½ cup shredded mozzarella cheese, divided

1 Tablespoon canola oil
1½ teaspoons Egg Replacer
1 clove garlic, minced
Sea salt and pepper, to taste

Preheat oven to 350°F.

Combine oil and vinegar to make a vinaigrette dressing. Brush both sides of each portobello mushroom cap with the vinaigrette. Arrange mushroom on a baking sheet, bottom sides up.

Bake mushrooms until tender, about 12 minutes. Drain any juice that has formed in the mushrooms.

Prepare Egg Replacer with 2 tablespoons of water. Stir well. Set aside.

Add garlic, sea salt, and black pepper together in a large bowl. Set aside.

Stir spinach, 3 tablespoons mozzarella cheese, and 3 tablespoons bread crumbs into the egg replacer mix until evenly mixed.

Divide spinach mixture over mushroom caps; sprinkle mushrooms evenly with remaining mozzarella cheese and bread crumbs. Return mushrooms to the oven.

Continue baking until topping is golden brown and cheese is melted, about 10 minutes.

Potato Skins

Makes 4 Servings

A party favorite that will please anyone in your crowd.

4 large russet potatoes, baked
1 tablespoon nutritional yeast
¼ teaspoon garlic powder
¼ teaspoon pepper
1½ cups Daiya shredded cheddar cheese
1 package Daiya havarti cheese wedge, softened

3 Tablespoons canola oil
½ teaspoon sea salt
¼ teaspoon paprika
½ cup broccoli florets, chopped
4 green onions, sliced

Preheat oven to 350°F.

Scrub the potato and prick it with a fork to prevent steam from building up and causing the potato to explode in your oven. Bake for 1½ hours. Allow to cool completely. Alternately, you can microwave potatoes until they are done, approximately 6-10 minutes, depending on their size and your microwave's wattage.

Preheat oven to 475°F. Grease a cookie sheet with coconut oil.

Cut potatoes in half lengthwise; scoop out pulp, leaving a 1/4-inch shell. (You can save the insides for another recipe).

Place potato skins on the cookie sheet. Combine oil, softened havarti cheese, sea salt, garlic powder, paprika and pepper. Reserve the cheddar cheese for later.

Bake for 7 minutes, rotate pan, and continue to bake until crisp, about 7 minutes more.

Add cheddar cheese and broccoli inside skins. Bake 2 minutes longer or until the cheese is melted. Remove from oven. Top with green onions. Serve immediately.

Cold Noodles in Spicy Sesame Sauce

Makes 4 Servings

If you cannot tolerate sesame seeds, you can make this recipe with sunflower seed butter and omit the sesame seed topping. I have even made this recipe with spaghetti squash instead of gluten-free pasta with success.

½ (8 ounce) package gluten-free spaghetti
1 Tablespoon agave nectar
¼ teaspoon red pepper flakes, optional
1 teaspoon ground ginger
1 green onion, chopped

2 Tablespoons sesame tahini
2 Tablespoons coconut aminos
1 teaspoon melted coconut oil
1 clove garlic, minced
2 teaspoons sesame seeds

Fill a large stockpot with water and bring to a rolling boil over high heat. Once the water is boiling, stir in the spaghetti, and return to a boil.

Cook the pasta uncovered, stirring occasionally, until the pasta has cooked through, but is still firm to the bite, about 8-10 minutes. Refer to package instructions if available. When done, drain and rinse spaghetti. Set aside.

Melt the tahini in a large microwave-safe glass or ceramic bowl, about 15 to 20 seconds (depending on your microwave). Stir in the agave nectar, coconut aminos, and chili pepper flakes, into the tahini, then add the melted coconut oil and ginger.

Mix in the garlic and green onions and toss with the spaghetti. Top with the sesame seeds.

Refrigerate at least 2 hours before serving cold.

Baba Ghanoush and Hummus

Serves 4

Baba Ghanoush is a delicious roasted eggplant dip that can double as a sandwich spread.
Both of these dips are great served with gluten-free pita (page 44) or raw veggies.

ooooooooooooooooooooooooooooooooooooooooooooooooooooooooooooooooooooooooooooooooo

Baba Ghanoush

1 medium eggplant
¼ cup tahini
2 cloves garlic, minced
1½ Tablespoons olive oil

¼ cup lemon juice
2 Tablespoons sesame seeds
Sea salt and pepper to taste

Preheat oven to 400°F. Lightly grease a baking sheet with coconut oil.

Place eggplant on baking sheet, and make holes in the skin with a fork. Roast for 30 to 40 minutes, turning occasionally, until soft.

Remove from oven, and place into a large bowl of cold water. Allow to sit for a few minutes to cool off.

Remove from water, and remove eggplant skin. Cut into large cubes and place in a blender. Add lemon juice, tahini, sesame seeds, and garlic, and purée. Season with sea salt and pepper to taste.

Transfer eggplant mixture to a medium size mixing bowl, and slowly mix in olive oil. Refrigerate for 3 hours before serving.

Hummus

2 cups canned garbanzo beans, rinsed and drained
¼ cup lemon juice
2 cloves garlic, halved
1 pinch paprika

¼ cup tahini
1 teaspoon sea salt
1 Tablespoon olive oil
1 teaspoon minced fresh parsley

Place the garbanzo beans, tahini, lemon juice, sea salt and garlic in a blender or food processor. Blend until smooth. Transfer mixture to a serving bowl.

Drizzle olive oil over the mixture. Sprinkle with paprika and parsley.

Lentil Paté with Gluten-Free Pitas

Makes 4 Servings

This simple recipe is a great way to get your protein and iron without having to worry about eating meat or taking supplements.

○○

Lentil Paté

2 cups vegetable stock
1 teaspoon extra virgin olive oil
1 cup roasted unsalted sesame seeds

1 cup dry lentils, rinsed
1 large onion, chopped
Sea salt and pepper to taste

Place vegetable stock and lentils in a large pot. Cover pot and cook about 30 minutes or until tender. Drain well.

Heat oil in skillet, and sauté onion until it becomes translucent.

In a blender or food processor, process lentils, onions, and sunflower seeds until your desired consistency for the pate is reached.

Season to taste with sea salt and pepper. Chill at least one hour before serving.

Gluten-Free Pita

1 package active dry yeast
1 teaspoon raw sugar
½ cup tapioca flour
2 teaspoons xanthan gum
1 cup warm water
1 Tablespoon ground flaxseed mixed with 3 Tablespoons warm water

½ cup warm water
1½ cups brown rice flour
1 cup sorghum flour
1¼ teaspoons sea salt

Dissolve yeast in ½ cup warm water. Add sugar and stir until dissolved. Let sit for 10-15 minutes until water is frothy.

Combine flours, xanthan gum, and sea salt in large bowl using a mixer. Pour in yeast mixture and flaxseed mixture and mix on medium speed using paddle attachment. Slowly add ½ -1 cup warm water and mix on medium for 2 minutes. Add enough water so that dough is soft.

Coat a large bowl with canola oil and place dough in bowl. Turn upside down so all dough is oiled. Allow to sit in warm place for about 2-3 hours or until it has increased in size.

Preheat oven to 400°F. Place baking sheet on the bottom rack. Create 12 small pieces of dough and place pieces on floured surface. Roll each into a circle, about 5-6 inches across and ¼ inch thick. Place several circles on the baking sheet and bake for 4 minutes, until bread puffs up. Turn over, and bake for additional 2 minutes until golden. Remove each from baking sheet with spatula and gently push down each puff.

Spicy Mexican Dip

Makes 6 Servings

A crowd pleasing dip that works well for chips, veggies, bread, and even a topping for rice.

1 (15 ounce) can refried beans
1 (15 ounce) can black beans, rinsed and drained
1 package Daiya havarti wedge, crumbled
1½ cups shredded Daiya cheddar cheese

1 cup salsa
¼ cup sliced black olives

Preheat an oven to 375°F. Grease a 1 quart casserole dish with coconut oil. Set aside.

Combine refried beans and black beans in the bottom of baking dish. Top with crumbled havarti, salsa, jalapenos, and shredded cheddar cheese. Sprinkle with black olive slices.

Cover dish, and bake for 15 minutes. While baking, prepare corn tortilla chips below.

Uncover, and bake until hot and bubbly, about 15 additional minutes. Serve with chips.

Corn Tortilla Chips

2 cups gluten-free masa harina
½ teaspoon sea salt, optional

1 cup of water

Mix masa harina with water until the dough starts to form a ball. It will be thick and heavy. Shape into small balls. Place each one between two sheets of parchment paper or a plastic bag and flatten it into a disc, about 5-6 inches in diameter. Cut with a pizza wheel into triangle or strips.

Prepare a large heavy skillet or deep fryer with oil. Heat to 375°F.

Test oil by dropping a small drop of water in the oil. If it begins to sizzle and pop right away, the oil is ready. Add a few corn chips to the oil at a time to not reduce the temperature, and fry about 30 seconds, until golden and crisp.

Drain on paper towels, and repeat until all corn chips are done.

Sprinkle with sea salt, if desired, while still hot.

Kimchi

Makes 8 Servings

Kimchi is a wonderful fermented spicy Korean vegetable recipe that most often contains napa cabbage, along with other optional items such as carrots, persimmons, or radishes. Allowing it to sit 3 or more days creates a natural fermentation and the end result is a kimchi loaded with natural probiotics. Traditionally, kimchi is served as an appetizer or topping to other foods. I like to have it with rice or on top of a salad, instead of dressing. Be creative and add other spices and vegetables to your kimchi. Make as mild or spicy as you like.

1 head Napa cabbage
3 cloves garlic, minced
3 green onions, minced
1 Tablespoon raw sugar
1 (1 inch) piece fresh ginger root, peeled and chopped

½ cup sea salt, divided
Red pepper flakes, to taste
2 Tablespoons water
1 Tablespoon coconut aminos

Cube the napa cabbage and rinse well. Put the cabbage in a bowl and sprinkle liberally with ¼ cup sea salt, tossing to mix. Set aside for 1 hour to wilt.

Mix the remaining sea salt into the cabbage and set aside for another hour.

When ready, wash and drain the cabbage. Pat dry.

Combine the garlic, ginger, coconut aminos, sugar, and green onions in a blender with the water. Blend on high speed until smooth.

Liberally add red pepper flakes to the cabbage, according to your spice tolerance. Stir in the garlic and onion mixture and stir well.

Transfer the mixture into sanitized airtight glass containers, packing them well and almost to the very top. Allow just ¼ of air space on the tops of each jar.

Allow to sit in a cool dry place for 3 days before serving.

Open jars slowly when ready to use, as the contents are under pressure and may leak.

Keep refrigerated for up to 2 weeks.

Cheese Sticks

Makes 4 Servings

This is one of those recipes that I simply had to do without until Daiya recently released their cheese wedges. I really like to use the havarti and cheddar in combination, but feel free to use any of their varieties. And yes, I have emailed them pleading for a mozzarella wedge, so cross your fingers!

○○

1 Tablespoon Egg Replacer
¼ cup water
1½ cups gluten-free seasoned bread crumbs
1/3 cup cornstarch
2 packages Daiya cheese wedges, any variety

2 Tablespoons rice milk
1 cup Free State flour, page 11
½ teaspoon garlic powder
1 quart oil for deep frying
½ teaspoon sea salt

In a medium bowl, mix together the Egg Replacer and rice milk. Stir well and set aside.

Mix the bread crumbs, salt, and garlic powder in a medium bowl. Set aside.

In a separate medium bowl, blend the flour and cornstarch. Set aside.

One at a time, coat each cheese stick in the flour mixture, then the egg mixture, then in the bread crumbs.

Place all cheese sticks in a freezer safe container or wrapper, and freeze for at least 4 hours.

When ready to prepare, heat the oil to 365°F in a deep fryer or large, heavy skillet.

To make sure your oil is ready, test by adding a small amount of water to the skillet or deep fryer. If it sizzles and pops immediately, it is ready.

Fry a few pieces at a time until golden brown, about 1-2 minutes. Do not cook too many, or you will reduce the temperature of the oil, and they will not cook correctly.

Remove from heat and drain on paper towels. Serve with marinara or your favorite dipping sauce.

Collard Rolls

Makes 4 Servings

I have a client who is so allergic to seafood that she cannot even have seaweed, so traditional sushi is off the menu for her. I invented this version of sushi for her, and I think that you will find it a refreshing change. Feel free to use another leafy green, such as swiss chard instead of collards, or use nori sheets if you can have seaweed.

1 cup uncooked short grain brown rice
1 pinch sea salt
1 Tablespoon brown rice vinegar
1 avocado, peeled, pitted, and thinly sliced
¼ medium red bell pepper, julienned

2 cups water
4 large collard leaves
¼ cup alfalfa sprouts
¼ cup shredded zucchini
¼ cup shredded carrots

Rinse and drain brown rice, place into a saucepan over medium heat, and pour in water. Stir in sea salt, bring to a boil, and simmer until rice has absorbed the water, about 45 minutes. Let rice cool until warm; stir in brown rice vinegar. Rice will be slightly sticky. Set aside.

To roll the sushi, lay a collard leaf, dull side up, on a flat countertop or other surface. With wet fingers, firmly pat a thick, even layer of brown rice over the leaf, leaving top edge about ½ inch deep uncovered with rice. Place 1 or 2 slices of avocado and a small amount of red bell pepper strips, carrots, zucchini, and alfalfa sprouts in a line along the bottom edge of the leaf.

Pick up the bottom edge nearest you, and fold the bottom edge of the leaf up, enclosing the vegetables on the bottom , and tightly roll the leaf just like you would a burrito, by now folding in the sides, and then around, into a thick cylinder. Once the leaf is rolled, you can hold with toothpicks if needed.

Ideally, eat collard rolls raw, but you can put in the microwave for 45 seconds to steam, if desired. I like to serve with guacamole and salsa, recipes on the next page, but you can serve any way you wish.

Guacamole and Salsa

Makes 6 Servings

I really love to serve these two together, whether with chips, the Collard rolls on the previous page, or as a salad topper. The mango really makes the salsa come to life.

◦◦◦

Guacamole

3 large avocados, peeled, pitted, and mashed
1 teaspoon sea salt
3 Tablespoons chopped fresh cilantro
1 teaspoon minced garlic

1 medium lime, juiced
¼ cup diced onion
2 roma (plum) tomatoes, diced
1 pinch cayenne pepper

In a medium bowl, mash together the avocados, lime juice, and sea salt. Mix in onion, cilantro, tomatoes, and garlic. Stir in cayenne pepper.

Refrigerate for at least one hour before serving.

Salsa

1 mango - peeled, seeded and diced
½ jalapeno pepper, seeded and minced
2 cloves garlic, minced
1 Tablespoon fresh lime juice

4 medium tomatoes, diced
¼ cup chopped fresh cilantro
1 teaspoon sea salt
¼ cup chopped red onion

In a medium bowl, combine the mango, tomatoes, jalapeno, cilantro, and garlic. Stir in the sea salt, lime juice, red onion, and olive oil.

To blend the flavors, refrigerate for about one hour before serving.

Antipasti

Makes 6 Servings

So much better, and better for you, than the original, which is loaded with fatty meats and cheeses.

○○

1 cup water
½ cup balsamic vinegar
½ cup lemon juice
2 Tablespoons fresh basil
1 large green pepper, cut into matchsticks
1 large red pepper, cut into matchsticks
1 cup green and/or black olives, pitted

1 teaspoon dried oregano
½ cup olive oil
2 Tablespoons raw sugar
1 broccoli crown, cut into florets
½ cup button mushrooms, sliced
½ cup chopped celery
1 Daiya havarti wedge, cubed

Add 1 cup water in a large saucepan or skillet. Add broccoli, peppers, mushrooms, and celery and bring to a boil. Reduce heat and simmer for 2 minutes, just enough to blanche but not boil or overly cook the vegetables.

Prepare the dressing by combining the vinegar, oil, lemon juice, sugar, oregano and basil.

Pour over the vegetables, add the olives, and let marinate overnight.

Just before serving, add cubed havarti.

Breads

Bread. The one food that I consumed most, and the one I was lease resistant to give up. Why? For the most part, gluten-free breads were hard to find, and hard to call bread because they were so very different than what I was used to. It was out of this necessity that I became a bread baker, and I am so glad I did.

While gluten-free breads are more available now at most grocers, there is a certain satisfaction to making your own bread. These are my personal favorites.

Focaccia

Makes 8 Servings

Focaccia is a seasoned herb Italian flatbread that is much thicker than pita or chapati. You can use it as a pizza crust, or serve along with a soup, salad, or vegetable dish.

○○

1 cup sorghum flour
½ cup potato flour
1¼ teaspoons sea salt
½ teaspoon garlic powder
2 teaspoons dried basil
1¼ cups water at 110°F
4 Tablespoons extra virgin olive oil
½ teaspoon of lemon juice
2 Tablespoons water

1 cup tapioca starch
2 teaspoons xanthan gum
1 teaspoon dried minced onion
2 teaspoons dried oregano
1 Tablespoon active dry yeast
A pinch of raw sugar
1 Tablespoon agave nectar
1½ teaspoons Egg Replacer
Cornmeal for dusting counter

Preheat oven to 375°F.

Combine the flours, gum, sea salt, onion powder, garlic powder, oregano, and basil to a large bowl. Stir well and set aside.

Prepare Egg Replacer with 2 Tablespoons of water. Stir well and set aside.

Add yeast, warm water, and the pinch of sugar to a glass measuring cup. Stir well and set aside. Double check the water temperature, as if it is too hot it will kill the yeast, and too low it will not allow it to activate. Allow it time to foam, about 10 minutes.

When the yeast is ready, pour the liquid into the dry ingredients and add olive oil, agave nectar, lemon juice, and prepared Egg Replacer. Stir to combine. The dough should be sticky and resemble muffin batter.

Grease a round cake pan with coconut oil and dust with cornmeal. Add dough, wet your hands, and shape into a rounded loaf.

Place the pan into the warm oven and turn off heat. Allow loaf to rise for 20 minutes. Remove loaf. Brush a small amount of olive oil over the top.

Heat oven again to 375°F.

Bake for 25 minutes, or until loaf is golden. Test for doneness by tapping bread. You may hear a hollow sound when it is done.

Chapati

Makes 8 Servings

Chapatis are thin flat breads that are eaten much like what we know in the United States as wraps. Use for sandwiches, burritos, or along with any meal or soup. Since we are not using yeast in this recipe, the temperature of the water is not as important, so you can bring it to a boil in a tea kettle, then add it when ready.

○○

1 cup amaranth flour
½ cup sorghum flour
2 teaspoons xanthan gum
1 teaspoon baking powder
1 Tablespoon agave nectar
3 teaspoons Egg Replacer
½ cup plain unsweetened rice milk

½ cup millet flour
½ cup tapioca starch
1 teaspoon sea salt
3 Tablespoons olive oil
1½ cups warm water
3-4 Tablespoons hot water
Coconut oil to grease the pan

Combine flours, gum, sea salt, and baking powder to a large bowl. Stir well to blend and set aside.

In a separate bowl, combine olive oil, agave, prepared Egg Replacer, hot water, and rice milk. Beat the wet ingredients into the dry mix with an electric mixer until the batter is smooth. It should look and feel like a thick pancake batter. This may take several minutes.

Heat a medium sized skillet or pancake griddle over medium high heat. Add a small amount of coconut oil to prevent sticking. Test the pan's temperature by adding a drop of water. When the water sizzles and bounces off the surface, the pan is ready.

Place 2 heaping tablespoons of batter into the pan and quickly spread the batter out as thin as you can. Let the chapati cook for a minute, or until firm. Flip over and cook the other side for a minute or until done. Repeat until batter is gone.

Multigrain Baguette

Makes 8 Slices

This is a great loaf to serve when you need a heavy, dense bread.

2/3 cup sorghum flour
½ cup millet flour
2 teaspoons xanthan gum
2 teaspoons dry Egg Replacer
1¼ cups water at 110°F
3 Tablespoons agave nectar
Sesame seeds for the top
Extra flour for kneading surface

1/3 cup amaranth flour
1 cup tapioca starch
1¼ teaspoons sea salt
1 Tablespoon instant dry yeast
1 teaspoon raw sugar
½ teaspoon cider vinegar
Coconut oil for greasing pan

Prepare the yeast by adding dry yeast to 1¼ cups water at 110°F. Add sugar, and wait 10 minutes for the yeast to proof. Set aside.

Mix together olive oil, agave nectar, and cider vinegar. Add to the proofed yeast.

Gently combine the dry and liquid ingredients to make dough.

Flour your countertop or other flat surface and knead dough by hand. You can omit this step and use a bread machine or a kitchen aid instead, following their instructions. After 3 minutes,
let dough rest 1 hour for rapid yeast and up to 2 hours for regular rise.

Punch down the dough and shape into a baguette. Sprinkle sesame and any other seeds/spices on top. Allow loaf to rise a second time, about 2 hours.

Preheat oven to 350°F. Grease a cookie sheet with coconut oil and place bread in center.

Bake 30 minutes on the center rack. Test for doneness by tapping loaf. It should sound hollow when done.

Naan

An Indian flatbread, much like pita, but shaped more oblong, like a wrapper.

½ cup warm water at 110°F
2 teaspoons active dry yeast
½ cup potato starch
1 teaspoon baking powder
2 teaspoons coconut oil
1½ teaspoons Egg Replacer
Extra flour for flouring the surface

2 teaspoons raw sugar
2 cups brown rice flour
½ teaspoon sea salt
1 teaspoon xanthan gum
½ cup plain coconut yogurt
2 Tablespoons water

Preheat oven to 450°F.

Place a heavy baking tray or pizza stone in the center of the oven to heat while you prepare the ingredients.

Combine Egg Replacer with 2 tablespoons of water. Stir well and set aside.

In a measuring bowl or cup, mix warm water with 1 teaspoon of the sugar and the yeast. Allow to sit in a warm place while you prep the rest of the ingredients for 10 minutes.

Combine the flour, starch, sea salt, baking powder, and gum in a medium bowl. Add the remaining sweetener, oil, yogurt, prepared Egg Replacer, and the water/yeast mixture. Blend until smooth by hand or with an electric mixer for about 1 minute. The dough will be very thick.

Divide the dough into six equal portions. Sprinkle some flour onto your rolling surface and the dough into a round shape about ¼" thick. Sprinkle more flour as needed onto the dough and/or the rolling pin to keep dough from sticking.

When you are ready to bake, carefully place each piece of dough onto your baking pan or stone.

Bake for 6 minutes, flip over and bake for another 4-6 minutes until they are very browned.

Dinner Rolls
Makes 12 Servings

It's amazing how as soon as you think you cannot have something, you miss it, even if you really never ate it much before. That's my relationship with dinner rolls. Now I like these better than traditional white rolls.

○○

1 cup brown rice flour
1/3 cup millet flour
1 Tablespoon potato flour
2 teaspoons xanthan gum
1 package active dry yeast
½ teaspoon fruit pectin
¼ cup cold water
1 Tablespoon plain coconut yogurt

¾ cup tapioca starch
2/3 cup sorghum flour
2 Tablespoons raw sugar
1 teaspoon sea salt
¼ teaspoon agar powder
3 teaspoons of Egg Replacer
1½ cups warm water at 110°F
2 Tablespoons olive oil

Heat oven to 200°F for five minutes, then shut off.

Grease muffin tin with coconut oil and set aside.

Prepare Egg Replacer with cold water. Stir well and set aside.

Place all dry ingredients except yeast, fruit pectin, and agar powder in a medium bowl and blend well.

Place prepared Egg Replacer, warm water, yeast, coconut yogurt, and olive oil in a bowl. Allow yeast to proof for 10 minutes.

After yeast has proofed, mix the wet into the dry ingredients. If using a mixer, use medium speed for 4 minutes.

Divide dough into 12 equal portions and place one into each muffin cup. Cover the muffin tin with a clean cloth and place in oven to rise for 20 minutes.

When the rolls have risen, remove from oven and preheat oven to 375°F.

Place muffin tin back into oven and bake for 20 minutes, rotating after 10 minutes, and continue to bake another 10 minutes or until golden.

Kalamata Olive Bread

Makes 8 Servings

I am a major bread freak, as well as an olive lover, so these two had to come together. This is my favorite bread to serve with salads.

½ cup amaranth flour
½ cup sorghum flour
2 Tablespoons flax seed meal
½ cup pitted kalamata olives, chopped
1 teaspoon sea salt
4 Tablespoons water
5 Tablespoons olive oil
2 teaspoons apple cider vinegar

½ cup garbanzo flour
1/3 cup tapioca starch
3 teaspoons xanthan gum
2 teaspoons active dry yeast
3 teaspoons Egg Replacer
¾ cup water at 110°F
2 teaspoons agave nectar
Coconut oil for pan

Preheat oven to 200°F.

Add the flours, yeast, and all other dry ingredients into a medium bowl. Stir in flax meal and combine.

Combine Egg Replacer with 4 tablespoons water, and stir well. Set aside.

Combine wet ingredients, including the prepared Egg Replacer, using a hand mixer or stir by hand. Slowly add dry ingredient mixture and mix with a wooden spoon until fully blended without lumps. When fully combined, add olives. Try not to break the olives as you stir.

Grease a loaf pan with coconut oil and place the dough into the pan. Use a spatula or knife to evenly shape the top of the loaf. Turn off the oven and place loaf inside. Allow the dough to rise for 90 minutes. It should rise to the very top of the pan.

Increase heat to 350°F and bake for approximately 40 minutes. The crust should be golden. Tap loaf to listen for a hollow sound.

Allow to cool slightly before removing it from the pan.

Irish Soda Bread

Makes 8 Servings

I am part Irish, and love having this, along with a simple meal of cabbage and potatoes, on St. Patrick's Day. It also makes a lovely breakfast bread. Since this is yeast-free, it is great to have any day for those who need or want to limit their yeast intake due to Candida or other conditions. If so, you can omit the raisins to make it more versatile.

1 cup garbanzo flour
½ cup potato starch
1 teaspoon baking soda
1 teaspoon sea salt
4 Tablespoons coconut oil
½ teaspoon lemon juice
¼ cup warm water
1 cup raisins
Coconut oil for the pan

½ cup sorghum flour
2 Tablespoons raw sugar
1½ teaspoons baking powder
2 teaspoons xanthan gum
¾ cup plain rice milk
1 Tablespoon Egg Replacer
1 Tablespoon agave nectar
Extra flour for dusting pan

Preheat oven to 375°F. Lightly grease a round cake pan and dust it with flour.

Whisk the dry ingredients together, including the powdered Egg Replacer, in a large mixing bowl.

Cut in the coconut oil using a fork or pastry blender.

Whisk the wet ingredients together in a separate bowl. Make a well in the center of the dry ingredients and slowly pour the wet into the dry ingredients. Add raisins and knead dough until blended, about 3 minutes.

Place dough into the pan and wet your hands to shape the dough into a round loaf.

Bake 30 minutes on the center rack of the oven, until the loaf is golden and crusty and sounds hollow when thumped.

Pizza Dough

Makes 8 Servings

I worked very hard to get a dough that would work for pizza, calzones, and similar goodies.
I make up a large batch and freeze it. It will last 3 months frozen.

○○

1 cup water at 110°F
1 Tablespoon raw sugar
1 teaspoon dried basil
1 teaspoon dried parsley
1 teaspoon sea salt
2½ cups Free State flour, page 11
Extra flour for dusting surface

1 package active dry yeast
2 Tablespoons olive oil
1 teaspoon dried oregano
2 teaspoons apple cider vinegar
½ teaspoon xanthan gum
Coconut oil and cornmeal

In a measuring cup, combine water, yeast, and raw sugar. Whisk together in a bowl and let it sit for 10 minutes or until it begins to foam.

In a large bowl, combine olive oil, spices, cider vinegar, sea salt, and xanthan gum. Stir well, then add the proofed yeast mixture. Add the flour, stirring in gradually until incorporated.

Oil a pan and sprinkle cornmeal on it to prevent dough from sticking.

Roll out onto a floured surface. Knead dough by hand for a few minutes. Shape into desired shape of crust round, square, or mini, and let sit 20 minutes. If you are freezing the dough, wrap in parchment or other good packaging. If you are ready to make pizza, continue with the instructions below.

Preheat oven to 425°F.

Bake the crust for 10 minutes. Remove from oven and add your sauce, vegan cheese, veggies, or any other desired toppings.

Return to oven and bake another 10 minutes, or until cheese is melted and hot.

Breadsticks
Makes 12 Servings
I certainly couldn't have pizza without breadsticks! When I am craving Italian, I go for these, along with some of my homemade tomato sauce (page 132) and then offset with a salad and soup for a well-balanced meal.

½ cup amaranth flour
1/3 cup tapioca starch
1 package quick-rise dry yeast
½ teaspoon garlic powder
1 teaspoon olive oil

¾ cup garbanzo flour
2 Tablespoons raw sugar
1 teaspoon xanthan gum
½ teaspoon sea salt
¾ cup water at 110°F

Mix together all dry ingredients. Stir in oil and warm water. Beat dough with electric mixer on high speed 2 minutes, or by hand. It will be somewhat wet.

Transfer dough to a large plastic bag with 1 corner snipped off to serve as a pastry bag.

Squeeze bag to create 12 breadsticks of equal size.

Cover and let rise for 30 minutes, or until breadsticks have doubled in size.

Preheat oven to 400°F.

Grease a cookie sheet with coconut oil. Bake 20 minutes on the center rack of the oven, or until dark golden brown all over and crisp on bottom.

Sandwich Bread

Makes 12 Servings

I really like to start my day with bread with some sunflower seed butter and a glass of coconut milk or coffee. I use this bread for breakfast, veggie sandwiches, and anytime I need a snack. Bake several and freeze them.

ooooooooooooooooooooooooooooooooooooooooooooooooooooooooooooooooooooooooooo

2/3 cup garbanzo flour
½ cup tapioca starch
2 teaspoons xanthan gum
2 teaspoons Egg Replacer
1 Tablespoon instant dry yeast
3 Tablespoons olive oil
½ teaspoon cider vinegar

1/3 cup sorghum flour
1 cup potato flour
1¼ teaspoons sea salt
1 teaspoon raw sugar
1¼ cups warm water at 110°F
3 Tablespoons agave nectar
Coconut oil and flour for surface

Combine the flours, starch, gum, sea salt, and dry Egg Replacer to a large bowl. Stir and set aside.

Prepare the yeast by combining raw sugar, yeast and warm water. Stir, and wait 10 minutes, or until it foams before proceeding.

Pour the liquid ingredients into the dry mix. Stir in oil, agave nectar, and cider vinegar. Stir to combine ingredients.

Flour your countertop, remove dough and knead for a few minutes. Return to bowl, cover with a cloth, and allow to rise for 2 hours.

Grease your pan with coconut oil.

After the dough rises, shape dough and add to the greased loaf pan. Allow a second rising time, another 1-2 hours. Dough should rise to the edges of the pan.

Preheat oven to 350°F.

Bake 30 minutes on the center rack, or until loaf begins to brown. You can test with a toothpick, and also tap the loaf. It should sound hollow when done.

Rye Style Bread

Makes 12 Servings

I was never a fan of white bread, and even as a child, I preferred wheat and rye. This was one of the hardest bread products to find a substitute that worked for me. If you were a rye fan like me, it's worth the time to try this one.

○○

½ cup sorghum flour
1 cup potato flour
2 Tablespoons unsweetened cocoa powder
2 teaspoons caraway seeds
1 Tablespoon active dry yeast
1 teaspoon raw sugar
1 teaspoon cider vinegar
1½ teaspoons Egg Replacer
Flour for your surface

1 cup garbanzo flour
2 teaspoons xanthan gum
1¼ teaspoons sea salt
1 teaspoon minced dried onion
1¼ cups warm water at 110°F
3 Tablespoons canola oil
2 Tablespoons molasses
2 Tablespoons water
Coconut oil for pan

Combine Egg Replacer and 2 tablespoons of water. Stir well and set aside.

In a large bowl, combine flours, gum, sea salt, cocoa powder, caraway seeds, and dried onion. Stir and set aside.

In a separate smaller bowl, prepare your yeast by adding dry yeast and sugar to the warm water. Allow the yeast to foam, about 10 minutes or so.

When the yeast is ready add oil, cider vinegar, molasses, and prepared Egg Replacer. Pour this blend into the flour mixture and stir until a dough forms.

Flour your countertop, and turn out dough. Knead by hand or use a bread machine or mixer for 2-3 minutes. If the dough seems dry add more warm water a tablespoon at a time. Cover with a cloth, and allow to sit 2 hours to rise.

After rising, punch down dough and knead again. Shape into the type of loaf you want and allow a second rising time, up to 2 hours, or until the bread approximately doubles in size.

Preheat oven to 350°F.

Grease the appropriate sized pan with coconut oil and place dough inside. Bake 30 minutes on the center rack. Test for doneness by thumping the loaf. It should sound hollow when done.

Ciabatta

Makes 12 Servings

Another popular loaf, this one was the favorite amongst the majority of my taste testers.

2/3 cup sorghum flour
½ cup garbanzo flour
2 teaspoons xanthan gum
2 teaspoons dry Egg Replacer
1¼ cups water at 110°F
3 Tablespoons agave nectar
4 Tablespoons extra virgin olive oil
Melted Earth Balance soy-free spread for the top

1/3 cup amaranth flour
1 cup potato starch
1¼ teaspoon sea salt
1 Tablespoon instant dry yeast
1 teaspoon raw sugar
½ teaspoon cider vinegar
Coconut oil for the pan
Flour for your surface

Prepare the yeast by adding dry yeast or rapid yeast to the water, then adding the sugar Wait 10 minutes for the yeast to proof.

Mix together the yeast mix with olive oil, agave nectar, and cider vinegar.

Gently combine the dry and liquid ingredients.

Flour your countertop, and turn out dough. Knead the dough by hand for 3 minutes. When done, return to the bowl, cover with a cloth let dough rest 1 hour.

Punch down the dough and shape into a long flat rectangle. Allow loaf to rise a second time, about 2 hours.

Preheat oven to 350°F.

Grease a cookie sheet with coconut oil and place bread in center. Brush with melted Earth Balance. Bake for 30 minutes. It should sound hollow when done.

Salads

Salads have the wonderful honor of being appetizers, sides, or main courses depending on what you add and how large of a portion you serve.

There is something for everyone here, as we feature an international blend of salads for year round eating.

Rainbow Salad

Makes 4 Servings

Together, these veggies offer not only a delicious salad, but a wealth of nutrients. The convenience of using any variety of kale as your green instead of lettuce is that kale does not wilt once dressed, so you can make this ahead of time and it will stay fresh for 3 days.

2 sweet potatoes, cut into 1-inch cubes
Sea salt and black pepper to taste
1 Tablespoon olive oil
1 bunch kale, torn into bite-sized pieces
2 Tablespoons red wine vinegar
1 small yellow squash, diced

2 Tablespoons olive oil
½ cup shredded red cabbage
1 small red onion, sliced
¼ cup dried blueberries
1 teaspoon agave nectar
12 grape or cherry tomatoes

Preheat an oven to 400°F.

Toss the sweet potatoes with 2 Tablespoons of olive oil in a bowl. Season to taste with sea salt and pepper and any other spices you enjoy, and arrange evenly onto a baking sheet.

Bake until they are tender, 20 to 25 minutes. Cool to room temperature before handling.

Once the potatoes have cooled, assemble your salad by combining all vegetables.

Prepare the dressing by combining the olive oil, vinegar, dried blueberries, and agave nectar Pour over salad and toss well.

Potato Salad

Makes 4 Servings

My taste testers really loved this recipe with the addition of the sliced green olives, but feel free to substitute sweet relish, black olives, or something "pickled" for that extra tang. This is definitely not your grandmother's potato salad, but I think you will find this is a recipe you pass on to others just the same.

○○

4 large russet potatoes, peeled and cubed
1 (14 ounce) can artichoke hearts, drained and chopped
1 package Daiya pepperjack cheese wedge, cubed
3 Tablespoons plain coconut yogurt
2 Tablespoons apple cider vinegar

½ cup green olives, sliced
1 teaspoon dried oregano
½ cup gluten-free croutons
2 Tablespoons Dijon mustard
Sea salt and pepper, to taste

Place the potato cubes into a large pot and cover with sea salted water. Bring to a boil; reduce heat to medium-low, cover, and simmer until tender, about 10-15 minutes.

Drain and allow to cool completely before handling.

In a salad bowl, lightly toss the potatoes, olives artichoke hearts, oregano, cubed cheese, Dijon mustard, vinegar, and coconut yogurt until all ingredients are coated with dressing. Season with sea salt and pepper.

Refrigerate at least 1 hour. Top with croutons just before serving.

Island Salad

A great summer salad any time of day.

1 small red onion, very thinly sliced
½ cup freshly squeezed orange juice
2 teaspoons melted coconut oil
2 cups small cantaloupe balls
1 ripe mango, cut into ¼ inch dice
1 large avocado
6 lime slices

2 Tablespoons red wine vinegar
1 Tablespoon grated orange zest
½ teaspoon Himalayan pink sea salt
2 cups diced seedless watermelon
1 cup loosely packed mint leaves
1 Tablespoon fresh lime juice
¼ cup shredded coconut

To make pickled onions, combine the thinly sliced red onion and the red wine vinegar in a small bowl. Cover; chill for at least one hour.

Pour the orange juice into a large salad bowl. Whisk in the melted coconut oil and orange zest and season with ¼ teaspoon of the sea salt. Toss the cantaloupe, watermelon, and mango in the dressing.

Dice the avocado into ½ inch pieces and place in a small bowl. Sprinkle with the lime juice, and season with the remaining sea salt. Stir gently to combine.

Spoon an even amount of avocado into the bottom of 6 small bowls. Stir in the pickled onions, coconut, and mint leaves. Top with melon salad and garnish each salad with a lime slice just before serving.

Marinated Tomato Salad

Makes 4 Servings

This is a simple but elegant way to use your garden tomatoes.

8 cups gluten-free bread cubes
1 cup minced fresh basil
½ cup olive oil
½ teaspoon sea salt
1 garlic clove, minced

3 cups chopped tomatoes
½ cup thinly sliced red onion
2 Tablespoons apple cider vinegar
½ teaspoon black pepper
A pinch of red pepper flakes, optional

In a large bowl, combine the bread cubes, tomatoes, basil, and onion. Set aside.

In a separate bowl, whisk together the remaining ingredients. Drizzle over the bread mixture.

Cover and let stand for at least 30 minutes before serving.

Spinach and Cranberry Salad

Makes 4 Servings

I really enjoy this salad year round, but especially in the Fall.

¾ cup raw sunflower seeds
1 cup dried cranberries
1 Tablespoon poppy seeds
2 teaspoons minced red onion
½ cup cider vinegar
¼ cup gluten free croutons

1 pound spinach leaves, rinsed
2 tablespoons toasted sesame seeds
¼ cup raw sugar
¼ teaspoon paprika
¼ cup olive oil

In a large bowl, combine the spinach with the sunflower seeds and cranberries.

In a medium bowl, whisk together the sesame seeds, poppy seeds, sugar, onion, paprika, cider vinegar, and olive oil.

Toss with spinach just before serving.

Red and Green Salad

Makes 4 Servings

I usually have this dressing on hand in the refrigerator in a glass bottle. It will last for about a week or longer if you omit the lemon juice.

○○○

2 Tablespoons sesame seeds
2 Tablespoons raw sugar
¼ cup raw apple cider vinegar
1 Tablespoon minced onion
1 quart strawberries, cleaned, hulled, and sliced

1 Tablespoon poppy seeds
¼ cup olive oil
¼ teaspoon paprika
1 head red leaf lettuce
Juice of one lemon

In a medium bowl, whisk together the poppy seeds, sugar, olive oil, vinegar, lemon juice, paprika, and onion. Cover, and chill for one hour.

In a large bowl, combine the spinach and strawberries.

Pour dressing over salad, and toss. Refrigerate 10 to 15 minutes before serving.

Pear Salad

Makes 4 Servings

Butter lettuce is also called Boston or Bibb lettuce, depending on where you live.

○○○

1 head Butter lettuce, torn into bite-size pieces
1 package Daiya havarti cheese, crumbled
½ cup thinly sliced green onions
½ cup sunflower seeds
¼ cup red wine vinegar
1½ teaspoons yellow mustard

3 pears - peeled, cored and chopped
1 avocado - peeled, pitted, and diced
Black pepper to taste
¼ cup olive oil
1½ teaspoons raw sugar
½ teaspoon Himalayan pink sea salt

In a large serving bowl, layer lettuce, pears, havarti cheese, avocado, and green onions.

For the dressing, blend oil, vinegar, sugar, mustard, sea salt, and pepper in a medium bowl, and stir well.

Pour dressing over salad, sprinkle with sunflower seeds, and serve.

Zucchini Salad

Makes 4 Servings

I usually serve this on a bed of Spring mix or turn into lettuce wraps using iceberg leaves.

4 cups thinly sliced zucchini
¼ cup thinly sliced green onions
½ cup olive oil
2 Tablespoons raw sugar
1 teaspoon dried basil

2 medium tomatoes, cut into wedges
¾ cup apple cider vinegar
1 garlic clove, minced
1 teaspoon sea salt
1 dash pepper

In a serving bowl, combine the zucchini, tomatoes and onions.

In a jar with a tight-fitting lid, combine the remaining ingredients; shake well.

Pour over zucchini mixture and toss gently to coat.

Cover and refrigerate for at least 2 hours before serving.

Asparagus Salad

Makes 4 Servings

I love to serve this salad with large baked potatoes for a hearty meal.

½ cup apple cider vinegar
1 teaspoon sea salt
¾ pound asparagus, chopped and steamed
1 package Daiya havarti wedge, crumbled
2 Tablespoons chopped cilantro

1 Tablespoon raw sugar
2 Tablespoons olive oil
1 large tomato, diced
Juice of 1 lemon

Whisk together the vinegar, sugar, sea salt, and olive oil in the bottom of a salad bowl.

Add the asparagus, Daiya cheese, tomato, green onion, and cilantro to the bowl with the dressing; toss to coat.

Cover and refrigerate for 1 hour before serving.

Lacinto Salad

Makes 4 Servings

This salad is in my opinion as a nutritionist to be one of the best meals you can feed your body. Feel free to add in other items, but do try to make with Lacinto kale when you can find it, as I find that yields the best flavor.

½ cup fresh lemon juice
2 Tablespoons raw apple cider vinegar
2 Tablespoons nutritional yeast
1 bunch lacinto kale, cut into bite-size pieces
¼ cup raw sunflower seeds
½ cup broccoli florets
¼ cup shredded red cabbage

½ teaspoon dried oregano
1 Tablespoon olive oil
Pinch of cayenne pepper
½ pint cherry tomatoes
½ cup dried cranberries
1 red bell pepper, diced
¼ cup shredded carrots

Whisk lemon juice, olive oil, nutritional yeast, oregano, and cayenne pepper in a large bowl. Set aside.

Add kale and all other items in a large salad bowl.

Toss with dressing. Serve immediately, or store up to 3 days in the refrigerator.

Sweet Escarole Salad

Makes 4 Servings

1 Tablespoon olive oil
Sea salt and black pepper to taste
1 large peach, peeled and sliced
¼ cup shredded coconut

2 Tablespoons apple cider vinegar
1 head escarole, cut in 1 inch pieces
½ cup raisins
¼ cup pineapple tidbits, drained

Whisk olive oil, vinegar, sea salt, and black pepper in a bowl until smooth.

Place escarole, peach slices, coconut, and raisins in a large bowl.

Drizzle with dressing and toss to coat. Serve immediately.

House Salad

Makes 4 Servings

This salad is a crowd pleaser that I serve with bread and my minestrone soup on page 78.

1 large head romaine lettuce
1 (14 ounce) can artichoke hearts, drained and quartered
1 (4 ounce) jar diced pimento peppers, drained
½ cup red wine vinegar
¼ teaspoon ground black pepper
1 green bell pepper, diced
½ cup Daiya shredded mozzarella cheese, optional
¼ teaspoon garlic powder
½ cup gluten-free croutons

1 large head iceberg lettuce
1 cup sliced red onion
½ cup extra virgin olive oil
1 teaspoon sea salt
½ teaspoon dried oregano
¼ cup sliced black olives
½ cup sliced mushrooms
¼ teaspoon dried basil
½ cup garbanzo beans, drained

In a large bowl, combine the romaine lettuce, iceberg lettuce, artichoke hearts, red onions, pimentos, mushrooms, green pepper, garbanzos, and shredded cheese. Toss together.

Prepare the dressing by whisking together the olive oil, red wine vinegar, sea salt, pepper, oregano, and basil.

Refrigerate until chilled and pour over salad to coat. Add croutons, toss, and serve immediately.

Fiesta Salad

Makes 4 Servings

This recipe features jicama, sometimes called yambean, which is a crispy, sweet, edible root that resembles a turnip. Jicama is excellent raw and is very popular in South American cooking. Most groceries stock jicama, so ask your produce department to help you locate it. Overall, this is an amazing salad, suitable to all eaters, and is a very filling meal.

ooooooooooooooooooooooooooooooooooooooooooooooooooooooooooooooooooooooooooo

1 head iceberg lettuce, shredded
1 bunch green onions, chopped
1 (15 ounce) can pinto beans, rinsed and drained
1 (15 ounce) can black beans, rinsed and drained
1 small green bell pepper, diced
1 (2.25 ounce) can sliced ripe olives, drained
1 teaspoon chili powder
½ teaspoon ground cumin
Cayenne pepper, to taste
1 Tablespoon olive oil
8 ounces shredded Daiya pepperjack cheese

1 small red onion, diced
2 large tomatoes, chopped
½ cup corn kernels, drained
½ cup diced red bell pepper
1 jicama, peeled and julienned
Corn chips, page 45
1 teaspoon garlic powder
½ teaspoon dried oregano
¼ teaspoon sea salt
¼ cup fresh cilantro
Guacamole and Salsa, page 49

In a large bowl, combine the corn, green peppers, red peppers, cilantro, onions, black beans, pinto beans, and all spices. Mix well to coat. Add olive oil, stir gently, and set aside.

In a large bowl, combine the lettuce, red onion, green onions, and tomatoes. Mix well.

Stir in the bean and corn mixture carefully, as to not mash the beans. Sprinkle with pepperjack cheese.

Before serving, top with guacamole and salsa.

Serve with gluten-free corn chips and additional guacamole and salsa.

Cabbage Salad

Makes 4 Servings

You can use the vegetables featured here with a tangy balsamic dressing instead of using the sunflower seed butter combination here for a flavor change.

1½ pounds green cabbage, coarsely chopped
1 small onion, diced
½ cup shredded carrots
1½ teaspoons minced fresh ginger root
3 Tablespoons coconut aminos
1 Tablespoon agave nectar
1 teaspoon sea salt

1 small red bell pepper, diced
2 stalks celery, sliced
4 radishes, sliced
¼ cup sunflower butter
2 Tablespoons lime juice
1 Tablespoon olive oil
¼ cup sunflower seeds

Toss all vegetables and fresh ginger in a large salad bowl. Set aside.

Whisk sunflower butter, coconut aminos, lime juice, agave nectar, olive oil, and sea salt in a separate bowl until dressing is smooth.

Pour dressing over cabbage and toss to combine.

Let stand at room temperature least 1 hour.

Sprinkle with sunflower seeds just before serving.

Green Bean Salad

Makes 4 Servings

If you prefer, you can omit steaming the green beans and serve them raw, which I often do in the summer or when I am having a raw foods day.

○○

1 pound fresh green beans, trimmed
1 pint grape or cherry tomatoes, halved
1 Tablespoon olive or canola oil
¾ teaspoon sea salt
1 cup chopped celery

½ cup thinly sliced red onion
2 Tablespoons lemon juice
1 Tablespoon water
¼ teaspoon pepper

Place beans in a saucepan and cover with water; bring to a boil. Cook, uncovered, for 8-10 minutes or until crisp-tender. Drain and rinse with cold water.

Place in a large bowl; add onion.

Place tomatoes in a separate bowl. Set aside.

In a small bowl, whisk together the lemon juice, oil, water, sea salt and pepper.

Pour over the vegetables in each bowl; toss to coat.

Cover and refrigerate for at least 1 hour.

When ready to serve, add the marinated tomatoes over the green beans.

Toss gently and serve.

Pink Salad

The beets and the red cabbage yield a pink juice in the skillet. I really like to serve this over roasted cubed potatoes or brown rice.

6 beets, peeled and cut into ¼ inch cubes
2 large carrots, julienned
1 bunch red Swiss chard, torn, stems discarded
½ cup red cabbage, shredded

1 jicama, peeled and julienned
1 cup frozen peas, defrosted
1small red onion, diced small
2 Tablespoons coconut oil

Place the beets in a saucepan with enough water to cover by 1 inch; bring to a boil. Reduce heat to medium-low, cover, and simmer until the beets are easily pierced with a fork, about 30 minutes.

Add the drained beets, red cabbage, and red Swiss chard to a large skillet. Add coconut oil, place over medium heat, and cook until the chard is tender, 3 to 5 minutes.

Stir in the peas and continue cooking until the peas are cooked through, about 5 minutes.

Place cooked vegetables on 4 serving plates.

Top with raw carrots, onions, and jicama.

You can add optional dressing, cheese, nutritional yeast, or other toppings of choice, if desired.

Sweet and Crunchy Salad

Makes 4 Servings

I enjoy this at breakfast, topped with Groovy Gluten-Free Granola, page 19

2 cups fresh pineapple, chunked
1 cup vanilla coconut yogurt
½ cup golden raisins

½ cup dried blueberries, chopped
½ cup shredded carrots
1 mango, diced

In a large bowl, combine all ingredients. Stir in the coconut yogurt until coated. Serve immediately. Refrigerate leftovers.

Soups

Soups are convenient, nutritious one pot meals that you can cook up and freeze for eating later in the week. Here are Free State's most popular soups. I prefer Imagine Foods brand vegetable stock for most of these recipes when I buy store bought, but you can simmer up your own using any leftover veggies you have.

Minestrone Soup

Makes 4 Servings

One of my favorite soups, Minestrone is a hearty delicious soup. Pair this with some focaccia (page ***) and one of our salads for a full meal.

3 Tablespoons olive oil
2 small yellow onions, chopped
5 medium carrots, sliced
2 cups water
1 cup canned kidney beans, rinsed and drain
2 cups baby spinach, rinsed
1 Tablespoon chopped fresh oregano
Sea salt and pepper to taste
1 cup garbanzo beans, rinsed and drained

2 cloves garlic, chopped
2 cups chopped celery
2 cups vegetable stock
4 cups tomato sauce, page 132
1 cup chopped green beans
3 small zucchinis, sliced
2 Tablespoons fresh basil
½ cup gluten-free shell pasta

In a large stock pot, over medium-low heat, heat olive oil and sauté garlic for 2 to 3 minutes. Add onion and sauté for 4 to 5 minutes. Add celery and carrots, sauté for 1 to 2 minutes.

Add vegetable stock, water, and tomato sauce, bring to boil, stirring frequently.

Reduce heat to low and add kidney beans, green beans, spinach leaves, zucchini, oregano, basil, sea salt and pepper. Simmer for 30 minutes.

Stir in the pasta and simmer soup until cooked. Serve hot.

Escarole Bean Soup

Makes 8 Servings

Escarole is very high in calcium and iron, and makes for a delicious green in this soup. Available year round, escarole is at its peak in the winter months, so I make up a large pot and freeze it around the holidays.

1 Tablespoon olive oil
8 cups vegetable stock
2 cups tomato sauce, page 132
Sea salt and pepper, to taste
2 (15 ounce) cans cannellini beans, rinsed and drained

½ cup gluten-free elbow pasta
1 head escarole, chopped
1 teaspoon dried oregano
1 bay leaf

Add all ingredients to a large stock pot and simmer for 30 minutes.

Discard bay leaf before serving.

Spinach Soup

Makes 4 Servings

Feel free to substitute chard, kale, or any other leafy green you have available.

6 cups vegetable stock
3 large potatoes, peeled and cubed
1 bunch fresh spinach, washed, roots removed
taste Red pepper flakes to taste

1 medium onion, chopped
¼ cup rice milk
Sea salt and black pepper to
1 Tablespoon olive oil

Add chopped onion and olive oil to a medium skillet, and cook over medium heat until soft, about 3-5 minutes.

Transfer onions to a large soup pot. Add stock, potatoes, sea salt, pepper, and red pepper flakes. Simmer until potatoes are cooked, about 15-20 minutes.

Add spinach, cover the pot, and turn off the heat. Allow to sit for 5 minutes.

Remove soup from heat, stir in rice milk , and season to taste.

Lentil Soup

Makes 8 Servings

This is a great soup to make on one of those hungry days, when a heavy meal is needed.

1 medium onion, chopped
2 carrots, diced
2 cloves garlic, minced
1 bay leaf
1 (14.5 ounce) can crushed tomatoes
8 cups vegetable stock or water
2 Tablespoons cider vinegar
Black pepper to taste

¼ cup olive oil
2 stalks celery, chopped
1 teaspoon dried oregano
1 teaspoon dried basil
2 cups dry lentils
½ cup spinach leaves
½ teaspoon Sea salt

In a large soup pot, heat oil over medium heat. Add onions, carrots, and celery. Cook until onion is tender. Stir in garlic, bay leaf, oregano, and basil, and cook for 2 more minutes.

Stir in lentils, and add vegetable stock/water and tomatoes. Bring to a boil. Reduce heat, and simmer for at least 30 minutes.

When ready to serve, stir in spinach, cover the pot, and turn off the heat. Allow to sit 5 minutes, or until wilted.

Stir in vinegar, and season to taste with sea salt and pepper, and additional spices of choice, if desired. Remove bay leaf before serving.

Sweet Potato Leek Soup

Makes 8 Servings

A new twist on a classic, using sweet potatoes adds to the intensity of this hearty soup.

3½ cups peeled and diced sweet potatoes
¼ cup finely chopped onion
3¼ cups vegetable stock
1 teaspoon black pepper, or to taste
5 Tablespoons Earth Balance soy-free spread

½ cup diced celery
1 cup sliced mushrooms
½ teaspoon sea salt, or to taste
2 cups plain rice milk
5 Tablespoons tapioca starch

Combine the sweet potatoes, celery, onion, and vegetable stock in a stockpot. Bring to a boil, then cook over medium heat until potatoes are tender, about 10 to 15 minutes. Stir in the sea salt and pepper.

In a separate saucepan, melt Earth Balance over medium-low heat. Whisk in tapioca starch with a fork, and cook, stirring constantly until thick, about 1 minute.

Slowly stir in rice milk as not to allow lumps to form, until all of the rice milk has been added. Continue stirring over medium-low heat until thick, 4 to 5 minutes.

Stir the milk mixture into the stockpot, and cook soup until heated through. Serve immediately.

Carrot Soup

Makes 8 Servings

I really enjoy this thick, creamy soup on the spicy side, but feel free to adjust the seasonings to your liking.

1 Tablespoon Earth Balance soy-free spread
1 cup cream of coconut (not coconut milk)
2½ cups sliced carrots
1 Tablespoon chopped fresh basil
½ teaspoon curry powder

1 Tablespoon tapioca starch
1½ cups vegetable stock
1 Tablespoon chopped fresh parsley
1 teaspoon cayenne pepper
Sea salt and pepper, to taste

In a large saucepan, steam carrots until tender in a small amount of water.

Transfer carrots to a blender or food processor, and add ¾ cup stock. Blend until smooth. Set aside.

In a medium saucepan, melt Earth Balance over medium heat. Stir in tapioca starch, parsley, basil, curry, and cayenne, and cream of coconut.

Cook and stir until slightly thickened and bubbly.

Stir in carrot purée and remaining broth. Season with sea salt and black pepper.

Simmer until hot. Serve alone or stir in cooked rice.

Squash Soup

Makes 4 Servings

I use butternut squash in this soup, but you can use kabocha (buttercup), acorn, or any other winter squash.

2 pounds butternut squash, cubed
1 Tablespoon coconut oil
½ cup plain rice milk
1 dash ground nutmeg
1 dash ground cinnamon

2 medium onions, chopped
4 cups vegetable stock
Sea salt and pepper to taste
1 dash ground cloves

In a large microwave safe dish combine squash, onions and coconut oil. Cover and microwave on high for 4 minutes.

Allow squash to cool, then peel off the outer skin.

Combine broth, squash, and all remaining ingredients except rice milk to a large stockpot.

Bring to a boil, then reduce heat and simmer for 25 minutes, or until squash is tender. Remove from heat and allow to cool for 10 minutes.

Purée soup in small batches in a food processor or blender. Add rice milk gradually as you blend the soup.

Return blended soup to the stockpot and heat until just boiling, then remove from heat and serve.

Ratatouille Soup

Makes 6 Servings
My favorite summer stew, in soup form.

3 cups tomato sauce, page 132
2 cups water
1 medium zucchini, cubed
½ cup dry gluten-free elbow pasta
1 teaspoon dried basil
1 garlic clove, minced

1 cup vegetable stock
1 small eggplant, peeled and cubed
1 large green bell pepper, chopped
1 teaspoon dried oregano
Sea salt and pepper, to taste
1 pinch cayenne pepper, optional

Add the tomato sauce, stock, water, eggplant, zucchini, green pepper, and all spices to a large stockpot. Bring to a boil over medium-high heat, then reduce the heat to low.

Cover and cook for 15 minutes.

Stir in the pasta. Increase the heat to medium and cook for 10 minutes, or until the pasta is tender, stirring occasionally.

Serve immediately.

Chayote Soup

Makes 4 Servings

Chayote is a South American fruit that when cooked, takes on a texture and flavor similar to summer squash. It looks like a folded pear, and is high in Vitamin C and Folate.

°°°

4 cups vegetable stock
1 small yellow onion, minced
¼ teaspoon red pepper flakes
2 Tablespoons chopped fresh cilantro

1 Tablespoon coconut oil
3 cloves garlic, minced
4 chayote squashes, peeled and diced
Sea salt and black pepper to taste

Melt the coconut oil in a large saucepan over medium heat. Cook the onion, garlic, and red pepper in the oil until the onion is soft.

Add the squash, cilantro, sea salt, and pepper, and stir frequently for 5 minutes.

Stir in the vegetable stock, cover and simmer on low for 20 minutes.

Pour the mixture into a blender and purée until smooth.

Pour into bowls and garnish with gluten-free croutons if desired.

Watercress Soup

Makes 4 Servings

Watercress is an herb that has a sharp, peppery and slightly sour taste somewhat like mustard greens. This herb is very high in vitamins, especially Vitamins A and K.

2 Tablespoons vegetable oil
1 medium onion, chopped
¼ teaspoon ground black pepper
1½ pounds watercress, large stems removed

1 medium potato, peeled and cubed
¼ teaspoon sea salt
2½ cups vegetable stock
2½ cups plain rice milk

Heat the oil in a large saucepan over medium high heat. Add the potato and onion, stirring to coat with the oil. Season with sea salt and pepper to taste.

Reduce heat to medium, cover and heat for 5 minutes.

Pour in the stock and the rice milk, and bring to a boil. Reduce heat to low and simmer for 10 minutes, or until potatoes are tender.

Stir in the watercress and simmer, uncovered, for 4 to 5 minutes, or until watercress wilts.

In small batches, transfer the soup to a blender or food processor and purée until smooth.

Return the soup to the pot, season to taste, and ladle into individual bowls.

Pinto Bean Soup

Makes 6 Servings

High in protein and iron, pinto bean soup is a great meal all by itself, or when served with one of our salads.

1¼ cups dried pinto beans
1 cup chopped onion
6 cups vegetable stock
1 teaspoon dried oregano
½ teaspoon sea salt
¼ cup chopped fresh cilantro

¼ cup olive oil
2 cloves garlic, minced
2 teaspoons chili powder
½ teaspoon ground cumin
¼ teaspoon black pepper

Sort and wash the beans.

In a large saucepan over medium heat, add the beans and enough water to be 2 inches above beans.

Bring to a boil for 2 minutes and remove from heat.

Cover, allow to soak for 1 hour and drain.

Add the beans, stock, water, chili powder, oregano, cumin, sea salt, black pepper and fresh cilantro.

Cover and simmer 1½ hours, or until beans are tender.

Pea Soup

Not only can dried peas help lower cholesterol, they are also of special benefit in managing blood-sugar disorders since their high fiber content prevents blood sugar levels from rising rapidly after a meal. As such, this is a great soup to serve to balance out a sweet item.

2¼ cups dried split peas
2 onions, thinly sliced
¼ teaspoon black pepper
3 stalks celery, chopped
1 potato, diced

8 cups vegetable stock
½ teaspoon sea salt
1 pinch dried marjoram
3 carrots, chopped
1 bay leaf

In a large stock pot, add peas and vegetable stock. Bring to a boil, then reduce heat and simmer gently for 2 minutes. Turn heat off, and allow peas to soak for 1 hour.

Once peas are soaked, add onion, sea salt, pepper, bay leaf, and marjoram. Cover, bring to boil and then simmer for 1½ hours, stirring occasionally.

Remove bay leaf. Add celery, carrots and potatoes.

Cook slowly, uncovered for 30 to 40 minutes, or until vegetables are tender.

Black Bean Soup

Makes 8 Servings

Black beans are so high in nutrients they are considered a super food, so I try to have them as often as possible. Loaded with magnesium, manganese, and a host of other trace minerals, black beans not only are good for you, but give you a food you can safely eat and enjoy without guilt or worry. For speed I use canned black beans here, but please consider soaking your own to lower the sodium content even more.

1 Tablespoon olive oil
1 stalk celery, chopped
2 cloves garlic, chopped
1 Tablespoon ground cumin
4 cups vegetable stock
1 (15 ounce) can whole kernel corn, drained

1 large onion, chopped
2 carrots, chopped
2 Tablespoons chili powder
1 pinch black pepper
4 (15 ounce) cans black beans
1 cup fresh diced tomatoes

Heat oil in a large pot over medium-high heat. Sauté onion, celery, carrots and garlic for 5 minutes. Season with chili powder, cumin, and black pepper; cook for 1 minute.

Stir in vegetable stock, 2 cans of beans, and the corn. Bring to a boil.

Meanwhile, in a food processor or blender, process remaining 2 cans beans and tomatoes until smooth.

Stir into boiling soup mixture, reduce heat to medium, and simmer for 15 minutes.

Serve immediately.

Middle Eastern Soup

Makes 8 Servings

Garbanzo beans, sometimes called chick peas or Bengal gram are loaded with magnesium, folate, copper, and protein. Often a staple in Middle Eastern cooking, such as hummus, they are mild tasting and work well in this soup. To make this soup more hearty, stir in cooked quinoa during the last few minutes of simmer time.

8 cups vegetable stock or water
1 medium tomato
1 large carrot
1 (15 ounce) can garbanzo beans, drained
1 teaspoon sea salt
½ teaspoon red pepper flakes
1 Tablespoon chopped fresh cilantro

1 medium green bell pepper
1 large yellow onion
1 baking potato, peeled
3 Tablespoons olive oil
½ teaspoon black pepper
½ teaspoon ground turmeric

Chop all the vegetables into medium chunks.

Heat the oil in a heavy pan, and sauté the vegetables together with the sea salt, pepper, and red pepper flakes for 2 to 3 minutes.

Add stock or water and garbanzo beans. Bring soup to a boil, then reduce heat and simmer for 15 to 20 minutes.

If desired, stir in quinoa or other gluten-free cooked grain of choice just before serving.

Thai Coconut Soup

Makes 8 Servings

This soup is a very rich and flavorful recipe. If you have difficulty obtaining lemongrass, you can substitute 2 Tablespoons of fresh lemon juice. Cream of coconut is thicker than regular coconut milk, but higher in fat and calories. If this is a concern for you, please substitute unsweetened plain coconut milk instead.

1 Tablespoon coconut oil
1 stalk lemon grass, minced
4 cups vegetable stock
1 Tablespoon agave nectar
½ pound fresh shiitake mushrooms, sliced
Sea salt to taste

2 Tablespoons grated fresh ginger
2 teaspoons red curry paste
3 Tablespoons coconut aminos
3 (13.5 ounce) cans cream of coconut
2 Tablespoons fresh lime juice
¼ cup chopped fresh cilantro

Heat the oil in a large pot over medium heat. Cook the ginger, lemongrass, and curry paste in the heated oil for 1 minute.

Slowly pour the stock over the mixture, stirring frequently. Stir in the coconut aminos and agave nectar, and simmer for 15 minutes.

Stir in the cream of coconut and mushrooms, and cook until the mushrooms are soft, about 5 minutes.

Stir in the lime juice; season with sea salt; garnish with cilantro, and serve.

Cream of Broccoli Soup

Makes 6 Servings

You can use frozen chopped broccoli in this recipe, but I prefer the slightly crunchy texture and bright green color of fresh. I sometimes use one of the other varieties of Daiya cheese for a change.

½ cup Earth Balance soy-free spread
2 cups broccoli florets, chopped
2 Daiya cheddar cheese wedges, cubed
1 Tablespoon garlic powder
1 cup water

1 medium onion, chopped
6 cups vegetable stock
2 cups plain rice milk
½ cup potato starch

In a stockpot, melt Earth Balance over medium heat. Cook onion until softened, about 5 minutes.

Stir in broccoli, and cover with vegetable stock. Simmer until broccoli is tender, 10 to 15 minutes.

Reduce heat, and stir in cheese cubes until melted. Mix in milk and garlic powder.

In a small bowl, stir potato starch into water until dissolved. Stir into soup; cook, stirring frequently, until thick.

Serve immediately.

Vietnamese Soup (Pho)

Makes 8 Servings

Vietnamese cooking relies on using many spices to turn simple ingredients into something very flavorful. If you like your food on the mild side, I suggest taste testing the soup to make sure you have the right amount of seasonings regularly. You can always add more vegetable stock if the flavors are too intense for you, but remember the noodles, when added to your bowl, will also help diminish the spice.

ooooooooooooooooooooooooooooooooooooooooooooooooooooooooooooooooooooooooooooooooooooo

Soup Ingredients

8 cups vegetable stock
2 medium onions, chopped
2 whole cloves
1 slice fresh ginger root
1 Tablespoon sea salt
1 pound dried flat rice noodles

1 small (daikon) radish, sliced
½ cinnamon stick
1 teaspoon black peppercorns
1 Tablespoon raw sugar
1 Tablespoon coconut aminos

Noodle Toppings

Chopped fresh cilantro
Thinly sliced green onion

Mung bean sprouts
2 Limes, quartered

Place vegetable stock, radish, onions in a large stockpot.

Tie cinnamon stick, cloves, peppercorns, and ginger in a cheesecloth or place in a spice bag; add to the soup.

Add raw sugar, sea salt, and coconut aminos to the stock pot. Simmer soup over medium-low heat for at least 1 hour (the longer the simmer time, the stronger the spices will infuse in the stock).

After an hour taste the soup, add sea salt as needed, and check the seasonings. If you are pleased with the flavor, discard spices.

Bring a large pot of lightly sea salted water to a boil. Add noodles and cook until soft, but not mushy, about 5 minutes, or as advised on the package instructions. Drain.

Place some noodles into each bowl, and top with a few sprouts, springs of cilantro, green onions, and a lime wedge. Ladle soup over the noodles and noodle toppings in each bowl.

Hot and Sour Soup

Makes 4 Servings

I really adore this spicy mushroom soup in the winter, but it is equally delicious anytime.

1 cup sliced shiitake mushrooms
½ cup diced bamboo shoots
½ teaspoon raw sugar
½ teaspoon ground white pepper
3 Tablespoons water
Red pepper flakes, to taste

4 cups vegetable stock
1 teaspoon coconut aminos
1 teaspoon sea salt
2 Tablespoons cornstarch
2 Tablespoons green onion
2 teaspoons cider vinegar

Place the mushrooms, stock, and bamboo shoots into a large saucepan, bring to a boil, and simmer for 10 minutes.

Stir in coconut aminos, sugar, sea salt, and white pepper. Simmer another 10 minutes.

Combine cornstarch with 3 Tablespoons water and add to the pan. Heat to boiling, stirring regularly, until thickened.

Stir in cider vinegar, then remove from heat.

Sprinkle with scallions and red pepper flakes just before serving.

Chunky Tomato Soup

Makes 4 Servings

I like to make this soup along with a Daiya grilled cheese toasts and salad for lunch.

1 medium red bell pepper, diced	1 medium yellow bell pepper, diced
8 large tomatoes, diced	1 (28 ounce) can diced tomatoes
1 (28 ounce) can diced tomatoes	1 medium onion, diced
1 clove of garlic, minced	2 cups vegetable stock
2 cups vegetable stock	1 teaspoon agave nectar
1 teaspoon sea salt	1 teaspoon oregano
1 teaspoon basil	1 Tablespoon cornstarch
1 cup plain rice milk	1 Tablespoon coconut oil, divided

Place the peppers in a stockpot with 2 teaspoons coconut oil, and cook, stirring constantly, until peppers are slightly charred, about 5 minutes.

Mix in fresh tomatoes, canned tomatoes, onion, garlic, and vegetable stock. Add seasonings. Bring to a boil, and cook 20 minutes, until tomatoes are soft.

In a small pan, heat the rice milk, remaining coconut oil, and cornstarch until thickened. Mix into the vegetables.

Remove half of the soup from the pot and transfer to a blender. Blend in small batches until smooth, and return to the pot.

Bring soup to a boil, reduce heat to low, and simmer 5 minutes before serving.

Beans

Beans are powerhouses of protein and other nutrients, perfect for those who adhere to a plant-based diet. Fairly low on the allergen scale, beans can be used liberally in your diet, and some varieties, such as garbanzo, can also be turned into flour for baking.

What I like most about beans is their versatility, and these recipes here span the globe. Canned beans are my guilty fast food, as I can open up a can, rinse them well, and toss them into a salad, mash into a burger, or add to a tortilla for a quick yet healthy meal.

Escarole and Beans

Makes 4 Servings

Cannellini beans are sometimes labeled as white kidney beans. You can use any other white bean in place of them if you prefer.

3 Tablespoons olive oil, divided
Sea salt and pepper to taste
1 clove garlic, minced
2 (16 ounce) cans cannellini beans, undrained

2 large heads escarole
¼ teaspoon red pepper flakes
3 sprigs fresh parsley, chopped

Heat 2 tablespoons olive oil in a large skillet over medium heat.

Toss in escarole, turning to coat with oil.

Season with sea salt, pepper, and red pepper flakes.

Cook, stirring occasionally, about 10 minutes, or until tender.

In a separate skillet, heat remaining 1 tablespoon olive oil over medium heat. Stir in garlic.

Pour in beans, and simmer until creamy, about 10 minutes.

Stir in escarole and parsley; simmer 10 minutes more.

Serve warm or cold.

Pumpkin Beans

Makes 4 Servings

The pumpkin that is featured in this recipe was at first a mistake in the kitchen, but wound up being such a pleasant surprise, I decided to keep it. Since pumpkin is very high in Vitamin A and several trace nutrients, it's a good item to use as often as possible.

1 small onion, chopped
2 cloves garlic, chopped
1 Tablespoon olive oil
1 cup peeled and diced potatoes
1 cup water
½ teaspoon black pepper

1 small green bell pepper, diced
1 Tablespoon fresh cilantro leaves
1 (16.5 ounce) can red beans, drained
½ cup peeled and diced pumpkin
1 teaspoon sea salt
¼ teaspoon cayenne pepper, optional

In a blender or food processor, purée onion, bell pepper, garlic, cilantro, and cayenne pepper. Set mixture aside.

Heat a large, heavy saucepan over medium heat.

Pour in olive oil and mix in beans, potatoes, pumpkin, water, and sea salt.

Reduce heat to low and simmer, stirring occasionally, for approximately 25 minutes, until mixture thickens and potatoes and pumpkin are tender.

Serve with gluten-free tortilla, or on top of rice or salad greens.

Baked Bean Casserole

Makes 4 Servings

This is the Free State way to make a hearty casserole out of meatless baked beans.

ooooooooooooooooooooooooooooooooooooooooooooooooooooooooooooooooooooooooooooooooo

2 Tablespoons olive oil
1 medium carrot, sliced
1 teaspoon raw sugar
6 button mushrooms, sliced
½ cup water
½ teaspoon dried basil
1 (14.5 ounce) can navy beans, drained
½ loaf gluten-free bread, cut into ½ inch chunks
¼ cup shredded Daiya cheddar cheese

1 large onion, sliced
2 cloves garlic, finely chopped
1 red bell pepper, diced
1 Tablespoon tapioca starch
1 Tablespoon tomato paste
¼ teaspoon dried thyme
½ teaspoon sea salt
¼ teaspoon black pepper
1 Tablespoon olive oil

Preheat the oven to 450°F.

Heat 2 tablespoons of olive oil in a large skillet over medium heat.

Add the onion, garlic and carrot; cook and stir until onion is tender and transparent.

Stir in the sugar, red pepper and mushrooms and continue to cook until onion is browned.

Sprinkle the tapioca over the vegetables and stir to blend.

Cook for 1 minute then mix in the water and tomato paste.

Season with basil and thyme. Mix in the beans and season with sea salt and pepper.

Transfer to a greased casserole dish.

Pour the remaining oil into a shallow dish. Dip one side of each slice of bread in the oil, then arrange on top of the casserole with the oiled side up. Sprinkle cheese over the top.

Bake for 10 to 15 minutes, until the bread and cheese are browned.

Aztec Beans

Makes 4 Servings

The combination of quinoa, black beans, and corn make this a healthy, but filling meal.

1 teaspoon olive oil
3 cloves garlic, peeled and chopped
1½ cups vegetable stock
¼ teaspoon cayenne pepper
2 (15 ounce) cans black beans, rinsed and drained
½ cup chopped fresh cilantro

1 medium onion, chopped
¾ cup uncooked quinoa
1 teaspoon ground cumin
Sea salt and pepper to taste
1 cup frozen corn kernels
Salsa and Daiya cheese, optional

Heat the oil in a medium saucepan over medium heat. Stir in the onion and garlic, and sauté until lightly browned.

Mix quinoa into the saucepan and cover with vegetable stock.

Season with cumin, cayenne pepper, sea salt, and pepper.

Bring the mixture to a boil. Cover, reduce heat, and simmer 20 minutes.

Add frozen corn into the saucepan, and continue to simmer about 5 minutes, until heated through.

Mix in the black beans and cilantro and heat until warm.

Serve immediately, topped with salsa and Daiya cheese, if desired.

Crock Pot Refried Beans

Makes 8 Servings

This is a really tasty way to make refried beans, without all the lard of the traditional.

1 onion, peeled and halved
½ fresh jalapeno pepper, seeded and chopped
4 teaspoons sea salt
¼ teaspoon ground cumin

3 cups dry pinto beans, rinsed
2 Tablespoons minced garlic
1 teaspoon black pepper
9 cups water or vegetable stock

Place the onion, rinsed beans, jalapeno, garlic, sea salt, pepper, and cumin into a slow cooker. Pour in the water and stir to combine.

Cook on High for 8 hours, adding more water as needed.

Once the beans have cooked, strain them, and reserve the liquid.

Mash the beans with a potato masher, adding the reserved water as needed to attain desired consistency.

Black Bean and Corn Quesadillas

Makes 4 Servings

This is a quick and easy way to satisfy your Mexican food cravings that the entire family will enjoy.

ooooooooooooooooooooooooooooooooooooooooooooooooooooooooooooooooooooooooooooooooooooooo

2 teaspoons olive oil
1 (10 ounce) can whole kernel corn, drained
1 (15.5 ounce) can black beans, drained and rinsed
½ teaspoon chili powder
¼ cup salsa, page 49
2 Tablespoons coconut oil, divided
1½ cups shredded Daiya pepper jack cheese

3 Tablespoons finely chopped onion
1 Tablespoon brown sugar
¼ teaspoon cumin
1 garlic clove, minced
¼ teaspoon red pepper flakes
8 (8 inch) gluten-free tortillas
¼ cup guacamole, page 49

Heat oil in a large saucepan over medium heat. Stir in onion and garlic, and cook until softened, about 2 minutes.

Stir in beans and corn, then add sugar, salsa, guacamole, cumin, chili powder, and pepper flakes; mix well. Cook until heated through, about 3 minutes.

Melt 2 teaspoons of coconut oil in a large skillet over medium heat.

Place a tortilla in the skillet, sprinkle evenly with cheese, then top with some of the bean mixture.

Place another tortilla on top, cook until golden, then flip and cook on the other side.

Melt more coconut oil as needed, and repeat with remaining tortillas and filling.

Veggie Chili

Makes 8 Servings

This is a very seasoned and filling bowl of chili, minus the meat. I like to serve this over rice or baked potatoes.

○○

3 (15 ounce) cans kidney beans, drained
2 (28 ounce) cans diced tomatoes with juice
1 large yellow onion, chopped
1 green bell pepper, seeded and chopped
2 green chili peppers, seeded and chopped
1 Tablespoon minced garlic
2 teaspoons ground cumin
1 teaspoon dried basil
1 teaspoon black pepper
1 teaspoon paprika
1 portion of corn chips, page 45

1 (15 ounce) can chili beans in sauce
1 (6 ounce) can tomato paste
3 stalks celery, chopped
1 red bell pepper, seeded and chopped
¼ cup chili powder
1 Tablespoon dried oregano
2 teaspoons gluten-free barbeque sauce
1 teaspoon sea salt
1 teaspoon cayenne pepper
1 teaspoon raw sugar
1 cup Daiya shredded cheddar cheese

Heat a large stock pot over medium-high heat.

Pour in the kidney beans, spicy chili beans, diced tomatoes, and tomato paste. Add the onion, celery, green and red bell peppers, and chili peppers.

Season with chili powder, garlic, oregano, cumin, hot pepper sauce, basil, sea salt, pepper, cayenne, paprika, and sugar.

Stir to blend, then cover and simmer over low heat for at least 2 hours, stirring occasionally.

After 2 hours, taste, and adjust sea salt, pepper, and chili powder if necessary. The longer the chili simmers, the better it will taste.

Remove from heat, ladle into bowls, and top with corn chips and shredded cheddar cheese.

Bean Burgers

Makes 4 Servings

This is simple and cheap way to make your own burgers. I use black beans, but you can use any beans you have on hand.

○○

1 (15 ounce) can black beans, rinsed and drained
½ cup water
¼ cup minced yellow bell pepper
1 large clove garlic, minced
½ teaspoon sea salt
1½ teaspoons Egg Replacer
3 Tablespoons olive oil

¼ cup quinoa
½ cup gluten-free bread crumbs
2 Tablespoons minced onion
½ teaspoon ground cumin
¼ teaspoon cayenne pepper
2 Tablespoons water

Bring the quinoa and water to a boil in a saucepan. Reduce heat to medium-low, cover, and simmer until the quinoa is tender and the water has been absorbed, about 15 to 20 minutes.

Roughly mash the black beans with a fork leaving some whole black beans in a paste-like mixture.

Combine Egg Replacer with 2 Tablespoons of water. Stir well to combine.

Mix the quinoa, bread crumbs, bell pepper, onion, garlic, cumin, sea salt, hot pepper sauce, and prepared Egg Replacer into the black beans using your hands.

Form the black bean mixture into 4 patties.

Heat the olive oil in a large skillet.

Cook the patties in the hot oil until heated through, 2 to 3 minutes per side.

Hawaiian Kidney Beans

Makes 8 Servings

These sweet and spicy beans are an excellent dish to bring to a BBQ or other event.

1 (8 ounce) can unsweetened pineapple chunks
1 Tablespoon cornstarch
¼ cup cider vinegar
1 medium onion, cut into wedges
½ medium sweet red pepper, diced
2 (16 ounce) cans kidney beans, rinsed and drained
1 medium tomato, cut into 1-inch cubes

¼ cup packed brown sugar
¼ teaspoon ground ginger
2 Tablespoons coconut aminos
1 large green pepper, diced
½ cup sliced carrot
1 garlic clove, minced
1 Tablespoon coconut oil

Drain pineapple, reserving juice. Set pineapple aside.

In a bowl, combine the brown sugar, cornstarch and ginger. Add enough water to reserved juice to measure ½ cup, if needed. Stir into cornstarch mixture until smooth. Add vinegar and coconut aminos and set aside.

In a large nonstick skillet, cook the onion, peppers and carrot until crisp-tender in 1 Tablespoon coconut oil. Add garlic and cook 1 minute longer. Add the beans, tomato and reserved pineapple. Cook for 2-3 minutes or until heated through. Stir in coconut aminos mixture and add to bean mixture. Bring to a boil, and cook for 1-2 minutes or until thickened.

Serve with rice if desired.

Black and Orange Stew

Makes 4 Servings

A sweet and tropical meal for the summer months, this black and orange stew is loaded with Vitamin C, which acts as a natural sunscreen in the summer.

1 Tablespoon canola oil
2 (1 pound) sweet potatoes, peeled and diced
2 (14.5 ounce) cans diced tomatoes with juice
1 small hot green chili pepper, diced
2 (16 ounce) cans black beans, rinsed and drained
¼ cup chopped fresh cilantro

1 medium onion, chopped
2 cloves garlic, minced
1 large red bell pepper, diced
1½ cups water
1 mango, peeled and diced
¼ teaspoon sea salt

Heat the oil in a large pot over medium heat, and add the onion.

Cook until tender, about 5 minutes. Stir in the garlic, and cook 1-2 minutes, until fragrant.

Mix in the sweet potatoes, bell pepper, tomatoes with juice, chili pepper, and water.

Bring to a boil, reduce heat to low, cover, and simmer 15 minutes, until sweet potatoes are tender.

Stir in the beans and cook, uncovered, until heated through.

Mix in the mango and cilantro, and season with sea salt. Serve immediately.

Bean Rarebit

Makes 4 Servings

Traditionally, Welsh rarebit or Welsh rabbit is a dish made with a sauce of melted cheese and various other ingredients served hot, and poured over slices of toast. I loved it when I was a vegetarian, pre-allergies, so it was one of the first recipes I worked on redoing.

○○○

¼ cup Earth Balance soy-free spread
¼ cup Free State flour, page 11
2 cups plain rice milk
2 cups shredded Daiya cheddar cheese
1 (15.5 ounce) can white beans, drained and rinsed

¼ cup chopped onion
½ teaspoon sea salt
1 teaspoon dijon mustard
8 slices gluten-free bread

Melt Earth Balance in a medium saucepan over medium heat. Cook and stir onion until soft, about 5 minutes.

Stir flour and sea salt into onion until flour forms a paste, about 1 to 2 minutes.

Gradually whisk in milk and dijon mustard into onion mixture and bring to a simmer, whisking constantly until the sauce thickens, about 5 to 7 minutes.

Stir in cheese and white beans into sauce until cheese melts, about 3 minutes.

Ladle sauce over slices of gluten-free toast or bread.

Kushari

Makes 4 Servings

Kushari is an Egyptian dish that features lentils, garbanzo beans, pasta and rice all on one plate. This delicious blend is one of my favorites to serve at holiday meals.

1 (14.5 ounce) can chickpeas, drained and rinsed
1 teaspoon ground coriander
½ teaspoon ground cumin
Water, to cover
1 pinch sea salt
1 Tablespoon olive oil
3 cloves garlic, minced
1 (14 ounce) can crushed tomatoes
½ (16 ounce) package ditalini or other small gluten-free pasta

¼ cup red wine vinegar
1 teaspoon cayenne pepper
1½ cups short-grain rice, rinsed
1½ cups dark brown lentils
Black pepper to taste
1 medium yellow onion, minced
1 Tablespoon coconut oil
3 cups vegetable stock

Combine the chickpeas, vinegar, coriander, cayenne pepper, and cumin in a sealable bag or container with a tight-fitting lid.

Store in refrigerator while preparing the remainder of dish, shaking occasionally.

Bring a pot of lightly sea salted water to a rolling boil. Cook the ditalini pasta in the boiling water until cooked through yet firm to the bite, about 8 minutes or according to package instructions. Drain and set aside.

Combine the rice with enough cold water to cover and soak for 20 minutes. Drain.

Meanwhile, combine the lentils with enough water to cover in a pot. Season with sea salt and pepper. Bring the lentils to a boil and cook at a boil until tender, about 20 minutes. Drain.

Heat the olive oil in a large saucepan over medium-high heat; cook the onion and garlic until translucent, 5 to 7 minutes.

Add the crushed tomatoes, season with sea salt and pepper, reduce heat to medium-low, and maintain at a simmer while you prepare the remainder of the dish.

Melt the coconut oil in a pot over medium-high heat. Add the rice to the oil, increase heat to high, and fry for 4 to 5 minutes, stirring constantly.

Pour the stock over the rice and bring to a boil. Season the rice mixture with sea salt and pepper, reduce heat to low, cover the pot, and cook until rice is tender but not mushy, and the liquid has been absorbed, about 20 minutes.

Mix the rice and lentils together on a large serving platter. Spread the cooked ditalini over the rice and lentil mixture. Top with the marinated chickpeas and the tomato sauce.

Lentil Loaf

Makes 6 Servings

It's all the comfort of meatloaf, but better, and better for you. Serve with any of our sides from the meal compliments chapter, and you're all set. I love this so much I selected this for the cover photo. It even works great cold as a sandwich.

1¾ cup vegetable stock
1¾ cups shredded carrots
1 cup chopped fresh mushrooms
2 teaspoons dried basil
1 cup Daiya mozzarella cheese
1½ teaspoons Egg Replacer
½ teaspoon sea salt
2 Tablespoons tomato paste

¾ cup lentils, rinsed
1 cup finely chopped onion
1 Tablespoon olive oil
1 Tablespoon fresh parsley
½ cup cooked brown rice
½ teaspoon garlic powder
¼ teaspoon pepper
4 Tablespoons water, divided

Prepare Egg Replacer with 2 tablespoons of water. Stir well and asset aside.

In a saucepan, bring stock and lentils to a boil. Reduce heat; cover and simmer for 30 minutes or until tender.

In a nonstick skillet, sauté the carrots, onion, and mushrooms in oil for 10 minutes or until tender. Add basil and parsley and sauté 5 minutes longer.

Preheat oven to 350°F.

In a large bowl, combine the carrot mixture, cooked lentils, cheese, rice, prepared Egg Replacer, garlic powder, sea salt, and pepper. Mix well.

Transfer to a 9x5 inch loaf pan coated with coconut oil.

Combine tomato paste and water until smooth and spread over top of loaf.

Bake for 45-50 minutes, or until a meat thermometer inserted into the center reads 160°F.

Let stand for 10 minutes before cutting.

Chana Masala
Makes 4 Servings

My love of India and its rich food and spirituality have been a part of my life for years, and with so many of their foods so easily adaptable to suit our needs, it only continues to grow. I prefer to use 2 cups dried chickpeas that I have soaked and cooked, but for the speed of it, I feature 2 cans of chickpeas here.

○○○

2 Tablespoons coconut oil
½ cup onion, chopped
¼ teaspoon garam masala
¼ teaspoon cayenne pepper, optional
1½ cups coconut milk
1 teaspoon cornstarch
2 (15.5 ounce) cans garbanzo beans, drained and rinsed

2 cloves garlic, minced
1 Tablespoon minced ginger
¼ teaspoon curry powder
1 large tomato, chopped
Sea salt to taste
2 Tablespoons water

Heat oil in a saucepan over medium-high heat. Stir in the garlic, onion, and ginger, and cook until browned.

Stir in the garam masala, tomato, coconut milk, and garbanzos; season to taste with sea salt.

Bring to a simmer, the reduce heat to low, cover and simmer until garbanzos are very soft, about 20 minutes.

To thicken the sauce, add 1 teaspoon of cornstarch to 2 tablespoons of cold water. Combine well, then stir into the chana masala.

Allow to sit for 2-3 minutes to thicken.

Serve over basmati rice, lettuce greens, or cooked potatoes.

Red Lentil Curry

Makes 6 Servings

Lentils come in several colors, but for this curry, I prefer to use red as they cook up faster than brown, and lend a nuttier, slightly sweeter flavor to this dish.

2 cups dry red lentils
1 Tablespoon coconut oil
1 teaspoon ground turmeric
1 teaspoon chili powder
1 teaspoon raw sugar
1 (14.25 ounce) can tomato purée

1 large onion, diced
1 Tablespoon curry powder
1 teaspoon ground cumin
1 teaspoon sea salt
1 teaspoon minced garlic
1 teaspoon ginger root, minced

Wash the lentils in cold water until the water runs clear in a colander.

Place the washed lentils in a pot with enough water to cover, and simmer covered until lentils become tender, generally 20 minutes.

While the lentils are cooking, sauté the onions in coconut oil in a large skillet until they become translucent.

While the onions are cooking, combine the curry powder, turmeric, cumin, chili powder, sea salt, sugar, garlic, and ginger in a mixing bowl. Stir well.

When the onions are cooked, add the curry mixture to the onions and cook over a high heat stirring constantly for 1 to 2 minutes, until well coated.

Stir in the tomato purée, reduce heat, and allow the curry base to simmer until lentils are done.

When the lentils are tender, drain if there is much excess water, and mix the curry base into the lentils. Serve immediately.

Tamales

One of my favorite Mexican dishes, tamales are steamed corn breads in husks, stuffed with beans and anything else you want to add. You will need good twine and a large pot with a steamer basket to make these. To reheat, steam or microwave until heated through.

Tamale Filling

2 cups refried beans
1 clove garlic
1½ teaspoons sea salt

1 large onion, halved
2 cups water

Tamale Dough

2 cups masa harina
1 teaspoon baking powder
2/3 cup Spectrum vegan shortening
1 (8 ounce) package dried corn husks

1¼ cups vegetable stock
½ teaspoon sea salt
1 cup enchilada sauce

Soak the corn husks in a large bowl of warm water.

Place onion and garlic in a medium skillet, and add enough water to cover. Bring to a boil, reduce heat to low, and simmer until the onion becomes translucent, about 5-10 minutes.

In a large bowl, beat the shortening with a tablespoon of the vegetable stock until fluffy. Set aside.

Combine the masa harina, baking powder, and sea salt; stir into the shortening mixture, adding more stock as necessary to form a spongy dough.

Drain the corn husks and pat dry. Spread the dough out over the corn husks to ½ inch thickness.

Place one tablespoon of the filling into the center. Fold the sides of the husks in toward the center and place in a bamboo or other steamer. Steam for 1 hour.

Remove tamales from husks and top with warm enchilada sauce and other toppings such as guacamole, shredded Daiya, sliced olives, jalapenos, etc.

Grains and Rice

There are several highly nutritious gluten-free grains available to you, some of which may be new to you. Quinoa, corn, buckwheat, millet, and rice are all great staples for their fiber and vitamins. Experiment with these in our recipes and those of your own, and balance them with veggies and beans for a satisfying and delicious meal.

Quinoa Tabbouleh

Makes 4 Servings

Quinoa is a versatile gluten-free grain from South America that makes a great substitute for couscous or added to any Middle Eastern recipe.

2 cups water
¼ cup olive oil
¼ cup lemon juice
1 medium cucumber, diced
2 small carrots, grated

1 cup dry quinoa
½ teaspoon sea salt
3 medium tomatoes, diced
2 bunches green onions, diced
1 cup fresh parsley, chopped

In a medium saucepan bring water to a boil. Add quinoa, reduce heat to low, cover and simmer for 15 minutes. Allow to cool to room temperature and fluff with a fork.

Meanwhile, in a large bowl, combine olive oil, sea salt, lemon juice, tomatoes, cucumber, green onions, carrots and parsley.

When ready, stir in quinoa.

Refrigerate for 2 hours to marinade, and serve alone or over a bed of salad greens.

Polenta Lasagna

Makes 8 Servings

This recipe is packed with veggies instead of meat and cheese. Using polenta instead of noodles is a delicious and lighter choice, so you won't feel overly bloated and full afterwards. Polenta works really well with tomato sauce, and I often use it as a medium for pizza toppings and other Italian inspired dishes.

3 medium carrots, sliced
1 large yellow squash, sliced
1 medium red bell pepper, chopped
4 Tablespoons olive oil
Ground black pepper to taste
4 cups water
1½ cups shredded Daiya mozzarella cheese

1 large zucchini, sliced
1 small red onion, chopped
1 cup tomato sauce, page 132
1 clove garlic, minced
2 cups cornmeal
1 teaspoon sea salt
Other spices, as desired

Sauté garlic, carrots, zucchini, squash, onion, and bell pepper in a large saucepan with a small amount of olive oil. Season with pepper and any other spices you like.

Sauté vegetables for approximately 5 minutes. Stir in tomato sauce, cover and simmer until vegetables are at your desired level of tenderness.

Bring water and sea salt to a boil in a large stockpot. Slowly add cornmeal, stirring constantly with a whisk. Lower heat and continue stirring for another 15 to 30 minutes until liquid is reduced and cornmeal is so thick it comes away from the sides of the pan.

Preheat oven to 350°F.

When ready, grease a 9x13 baking pan with coconut oil.

Spread cornmeal evenly in the pan. Spoon the vegetable mixture over the polenta and then sprinkle with Mozzarella cheese. Cover pan with aluminum foil.

Bake casserole for 30 minutes on the center rack of the oven. Remove from oven and let cool for 5 minutes before serving.

Southern Red Rice

Makes 8 Servings

This spicy recipe is delicious as a side dish or main course.

1 cup tomato sauce, page 132
1 large onion, chopped
2 Tablespoons minced garlic
2 cups long grain white rice
¼ teaspoon cayenne pepper
1 Tablespoon dried parsley

¼ cup olive oil
1 green bell pepper, chopped
2 stalks celery, chopped
1 teaspoon dried thyme
4 cups water
2 cups long grain white rice

In a skillet, heat oil over medium heat. Cook onions, peppers, garlic, and celery in olive oil for 3 to 4 minutes.

In a saucepan, bring water and rice to a boil.

Reduce heat, cover, and simmer for 20 minutes until all water is absorbed.

Stir in tomato sauce, and season with cayenne pepper, thyme, and parsley.

Simmer for 10 minutes.

Stuffed Portabellas

Makes 4 Servings

The combination of buckwheat kasha, also called buckwheat groats, and mushrooms is delicious, and I enjoy this meal as a substitute for turkey and stuffing on Thanksgiving.

ooooooooooooooooooooooooooooooooooooooooooooooooooooooooooooooooooooooooooooooooooooooo

4 large portabella mushrooms
Sea salt and black pepper, to taste
1 cup chopped fresh cilantro
1 stalk celery, finely chopped
1¼ cups vegetable stock

2 Tablespoons olive oil, divided
1 clove garlic, minced
1 large carrot, finely chopped
2/3 cup kasha
3 Tablespoons fresh parsley

Preheat the oven to 400°F.

Remove the mushroom stems from the caps, and set the stems aside.

Place the caps gill-side up on a baking sheet.

Drizzle with 1 tablespoon of olive oil, and season with sea salt and pepper. Roast on the center rack of the oven for 25 minutes.

Meanwhile, prepare the pilaf.

Chop mushroom stems. Heat the remaining olive oil in a skillet over medium heat. Cook stems and garlic in oil until soft, about 10 minutes. Stir in the cilantro, carrot, celery and kasha and cook 2 minutes more. Pour in water. Bring the mixture to a boil, reduce heat to low, and place a lid on the pan. Simmer for 20 minutes, or until the kasha is tender. Remove from the heat, and stir in parsley.

Season to taste with sea salt and pepper.

Stuff the warm mushroom caps with the pilaf, and serve.

Mushroom Risotto

Makes 4 Servings

This creamy, cheesy rice makes a great stuffing for peppers, cabbage, or mushrooms. My favorite way to serve mushroom risotto is with eggplant parmesan for a special meal.

1 Tablespoon olive oil
1 clove garlic, crushed
1 teaspoon minced celery
1½ cups sliced fresh mushrooms
¼ cup cream of coconut
5 cups vegetable stock
1 cup Daiya shredded mozzarella cheese

3 small onions, finely chopped
1 teaspoon minced fresh parsley
Sea salt and pepper to taste
1 cup plain coconut milk
1 cup Arborio rice
1 teaspoon coconut oil

Heat olive oil in a large skillet over medium-high heat. Sauté the onion and garlic in the olive oil until onion is tender and garlic is lightly browned.

Remove garlic, and stir in the parsley, celery, sea salt, and pepper. Cook until celery is tender, then add the mushrooms.

Reduce heat to low, and continue cooking until the mushrooms are soft.

Pour the coconut milk and cream of coconut into the skillet, and stir in the rice. Heat to a simmer. Add the vegetable stock into the rice one cup at a time, stirring constantly, until it is absorbed. This can take some time, so do be patient.

When the rice has finished cooking, stir in the coconut oil and mozzarella cheese, and remove from heat. Serve hot.

Spanish Rice
Makes 4 Servings

This is one of my mother's recipes that I expanded on. She made simple meals but did not use a lot of herbs or spices, so instead of sausage I added some additional flavor.

½ cup red onion, finely chopped
1 (14.5 ounce) can canned tomatoes
¾ cup uncooked long grain rice
1 teaspoon brown sugar
½ cup Daiya shredded cheddar cheese
2 Tablespoons chopped fresh cilantro
Coconut oil to grease pan

¼ cup green bell pepper, diced
1 cup vegetable stock
1 teaspoon sea salt
½ teaspoon ground cumin
1 pinch black pepper
A pinch of red pepper flakes
2 Tablespoons olive oil

Preheat oven to 375°F.

Heat oil in a large skillet over medium-high heat. Stir in the onion, green bell pepper, tomatoes, water, rice, red pepper flakes, sea salt, brown sugar, cumin, and black pepper. Simmer for 30 minutes, stirring occasionally, until much of the liquid has been absorbed.

Transfer rice to a 2-quart casserole dish greased with coconut oil. Press down firmly and sprinkle with the cheese.

Bake on the center rack for 15 minutes, or until cheese is melted and bubbly.

Garnish with chopped fresh cilantro.

Biryani

Makes 4 Servings

A traditional Indian rice dish, Biryani can be made simple or quite elegantly with additional vegetables and seasonings. Usually served as a side dish with other meals, Biryani is especially good with a lentil or curry dish.

2 Tablespoons coconut oil
½ teaspoon cumin seeds
1 Tablespoon ground ginger
½ cup vegetable stock
½ cup diced carrot
1 teaspoon sea salt
¼ teaspoon black pepper
¼ teaspoon ground turmeric
2 cups basmati rice, rinsed and drained

1 small red onion, diced
1 (1 inch) piece cinnamon stick
1 large tomato, diced
½ cup peas, thawed
½ cup diced potato
¼ teaspoon cayenne pepper
½ teaspoon garam masala
4 cups water

Melt coconut oil in a large Dutch oven over medium heat. Add onion, and cook until softened, about 3 minutes.

Stir in cumin seeds and cinnamon stick, and cook until the spices are fragrant, and the cumin seeds begin to pop, about 3 minutes.

Stir in ginger, tomatoes, and vegetable stock. Bring to a simmer, and cook until the stock has evaporated, about 5 minutes.

Stir in peas, carrot, and potato. Season with sea salt, cayenne, black pepper, garam masala, and turmeric. Stir well, then cover, and cook for 3 minutes.

Pour in 4 cups water and bring to a boil over high heat.

Once boiling, stir in basmati rice, reduce heat to medium, recover, and simmer for 10 minutes.

Reduce heat to low and continue to cook until the rice has softened, 10 to 15 minutes more.

Fried Rice Bowl

Makes 4 Servings

A simple and tasty meal, feel free to substitute seasonal vegetables on hand.

1½ cups vegetable stock
3 Tablespoons coconut oil
½ pound fresh asparagus, trimmed and cut
1 large yellow onion, sliced
2 teaspoons minced fresh ginger root

¾ cup long-grain white rice
3 Tablespoons coconut aminos
1 large red bell pepper, sliced
2 cups sliced mushrooms
1 teaspoon minced garlic

Preheat oven to 350°F.

In a saucepan combine stock, rice and one tablespoon of coconut oil. Cover and bring to a boil over high heat.

Reduce heat to low and simmer for 15 minutes, or until all liquid is absorbed.

Meanwhile, heat remaining coconut oil in a large skillet or wok over medium-high heat until very hot.

Add asparagus, bell pepper, onion, mushrooms, ginger and garlic and stir-fry for 4 to 5 minutes, or until vegetables are tender but crisp.

Stir in coconut aminos and cook for 30 seconds.

Serve hot.

Quinoa Curry

Leftovers are fantastic wrapped in a gluten-free wrapper, topped with salad veggies as a hearty lunch.

ooooooooooooooooooooooooooooooooooooooooooooooooooooooooooooooooooooooooooooooo

2 Tablespoons coconut oil
2 cloves garlic, minced
2 cups vegetable stock
Sea salt and pepper to taste
1 small carrot, diced

1 small onion, diced
1 cup quinoa
1 Tablespoon curry powder
1 cup cauliflower florets

Heat oil in a large skillet over medium heat. Add onion and garlic and cook and stir for 2 minutes; add quinoa and cook and stir until lightly toasted, about 5 minutes.

Pour stock into the pan and bring to a boil.

Reduce heat and add curry, cover, and simmer until tender, about 25 minutes.

Add cauliflower and carrot to the pan for the last 5 minutes of cooking time.

Season to taste with sea salt and pepper, fluff with a fork, and serve.

Quinoa Burgers

Makes 5 Servings

These burgers are very versatile and are liked even by those who would otherwise not eat gluten-free, vegan, or allergy-free.

1 (15 ounce) can chickpeas, rinsed and drained
½ cup vegetable stock
¼ cup minced yellow bell pepper
1 large clove garlic, minced
½ teaspoon sea salt
2 Tablespoons water

¼ cup quinoa
½ cup gluten-free bread crumbs
2 Tablespoons minced onion
1 teaspoon ground cumin
1½ teaspoons Egg Replacer
3 Tablespoons olive oil

Bring the quinoa and stock to a boil in a saucepan.

Reduce heat to medium-low, cover, and simmer until the quinoa is tender and the liquid has been absorbed, about 15 to 20 minutes.

Roughly mash the chickpeas with a fork, leaving some beans whole. The texture should resemble lumpy refried beans.

Mix the quinoa, bread crumbs, bell pepper, onion, garlic, cumin, and sea salt, into the beans using your hands.

Mix Egg Replacer with water. Stir well, and add. Blend well.

Form the mixture into 5 patties.

Heat the olive oil in a large skillet.

Cook the patties in the hot oil until heated through, 2 to 3 minutes per side.

Serve on a gluten-free bun or crumbled in a wrapper, topped with your favorite burger toppings.

Millet Italiano

Makes 4 Servings

This is a recipe remake that one of my college roommates made using cous cous. I actually prefer it with millet.

ooooooooooooooooooooooooooooooooooooooooooooooooooooooooooooooooooooooooooooooooooooooooooo

1 cup millet
5 medium bell peppers, sliced thickly
2 cups tomato sauce, page 132

4 cups vegetable stock
3 medium tomatoes, chopped
2 Tablespoons olive oil

Heat oil in a large skillet. Add peppers and cook on low-medium, until they become bright green, about 10 minutes.

Stir in tomato sauce, cover, and reduce heat to low. Simmer until soft, about 20 minutes.

While this simmers, combine the millet and vegetable stock in a saucepan, and bring to a boil. Reduce heat to low, cover, and simmer for 15 minutes, or until the water is absorbed.

Stir the couscous into the tomato sauce gradually, until well coated. Simmer for 15 minutes.

Eat as is, or use the quinoa as a stuffing for cabbage, mushrooms, or squash.

Polenta Risotto

Makes 4 Servings

This is a real comfort food meal that I make frequently for guests. I like to serve it topped with sautéed spinach and kale with just a splash of tomato sauce on top.

1 cup kernel corn, fresh or thawed
1 teaspoon minced garlic
3 cups water
1 cup cornmeal
½ cup Daiya shredded mozzarella cheese

3 Tablespoons olive oil
½ small onion, diced
2 cups plain rice milk
Sea salt and pepper to taste

In a heavy 4-quart saucepan heat oil over medium heat. Stir in garlic and onions; reduce heat to low and cook until onions are translucent.

Stir in water and rice milk and bring to a boil over medium-high heat. Slowly stir in cornmeal, whisking continuously to help prevent lumps.

Reduce heat to low and simmer for 30 minutes, stirring often to prevent sticking and burning.

Season with sea salt and pepper; simmer 15 minutes more.

When cornmeal is tender, stir in corn and mozzarella cheese.

Transfer to a large bowl to serve.

Corncakes

Makes 4 Servings

This is a versatile meal that serves well any time of the day, sweet or savory.

1 cup corn meal
4½ teaspoons baking powder
½ teaspoon sea salt
4 Tablespoons water
2 Tablespoons melted coconut oil

2/3 cup Free State flour, page 11
2 teaspoons raw sugar
1 Tablespoon Egg Replacer
1¼ cups plain rice milk
Coconut oil for the pan

Prepare Egg Replacer with water. Stir well and set aside.

Stir together the remaining dry ingredients in a bowl. Set aside.

Combine the Egg Replacer and rice milk together in a large bowl. Gradually beat in the dry ingredients and, when well combined, stir in the melted coconut oil.

Heat a griddle or heavy skillet and add enough coconut oil to coat. Using a tablespoon, add enough batter to make cakes 2 inches in diameter.

Cook for 2 minutes, until the bottom is golden brown, then turn over and cook the other side until cooked through, about 2-3 minutes

Serve the cakes straight from the griddle topped with salsa, veggies, or cheese for a savory meal or with maple syrup and fruit for a sweet dish.

Kasha Leek Casserole

Makes 4 Servings

Easy to make, this casserole is good alone or served with a green salad.

1 cup whole buckwheat kasha
2 Tablespoons water
1 large leek, white portion only, sliced
1 cup green peas, thawed
Sea salt and pepper to taste

1½ teaspoons Egg Replacer
2 cups vegetable stock
1 cup sliced mushrooms
2 teaspoons coconut aminos
Coconut oil for cooking

Prepare Egg Replacer with 2 tablespoons of water. Stir well and set aside.

Heat a saucepan to low-medium and add stock, kasha, coconut aminos, sea salt and pepper. Stir well. Cover and let simmer for 20-25 minutes or until all liquid is absorbed.

While this cooks, sauté leeks and mushrooms for about 5 minutes in a small amount of coconut oil. Add peas and cook another 5 minutes.

Remove kasha from heat. Stir in vegetables and allow to sit a few minutes before serving.

Green Millet

Makes 4 Servings

Easy to make, this casserole is good alone or served with a green salad.

○○

½ head green cabbage, shredded
1 small onion, chopped
2 teaspoons coconut aminos
2 cups vegetable stock
Sea salt and pepper, to taste

3 baby bok choy, chopped
1 cup dry millet
Red pepper flakes, optional
Coconut oil for pan

Bring stock to a boil. Stir in millet, reduce heat, and simmer until soft, about 20-15 minutes, stirring frequently.

Heat coconut oil in a large skillet.

Quickly sauté all ingredients, including the millet, for about 5 minutes, or until they achieve the desired level of tenderness.

Serve immediately.

Italian Rice Balls

Very versatile, these rice balls can be used instead of meatballs, topped with cheese for a parmesan treat, or as an appetizer.

2 cups cooked white or brown rice
1½ teaspoons Egg Replacer
Sea salt and pepper, to taste
1½ teaspoons mustard powder
2 teaspoons paprika
½ teaspoon basil

¾ cup shredded Daiya cheddar cheese
2 Tablespoons water
¼ teaspoon onion powder
1 cup gluten-free breadcrumbs
½ teaspoon oregano

Combine Egg Replacer and water. Stir well and set aside.

Combine all ingredients except bread crumbs and spices. Chill for at least one hour.

Form rice into small balls using 1 Tablespoon of mixture for each.

Blend crumbs and spices to season. Roll balls in seasoned crumbs until well coated.

Heat oil in a large skillet or deep fryer to 375°F. Test oil by dropping a small amount of water into the pan. If its spits immediately, it is ready.

Fry in small batches, about 3 minutes. Drain.

Serve with optional marinara or other desired dipping sauces.

Pasta and Noodles

As a vegan, pasta and noodles had been a huge part of my cooking repertoire, especially when cooking for others. When it came to removing wheat and gluten, I was at a loss initially. Now, with my own homemade pasta dough recipe on page 138, plus the many new gluten-free varieties of packaged pasta available, my pasta and noodle dishes are back, better than ever.

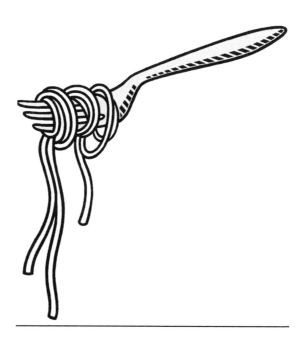

Macaroni and Cheese

Makes 4 Servings

For me, this is the ultimate comfort food and one of the meals I enjoy most. Thanks to Daiya, this recipe is possible again. Whenever I make it, I get compliments from those who never suspect its vegan, gluten-free, and allergy-safe as well.

8 ounces gluten-free pasta, any shape
1 package Daiya havarti wedge, diced
2 Tablespoons Earth Balance soy-free spread
¼ teaspoon paprika

3 cups shredded Daiya cheddar cheese
1 cup plain rice milk
¼ cup nutritional yeast
¼ cup plain coconut yogurt

Cook pasta according to package instructions, being careful to not overcook. Drain pasta and set aside.

In a large stockpot, melt Earth Balance. Add rice milk, paprika, and cheddar cheese.

Cook on low-medium heat until melted, stirring frequently. When melted, stir in the havarti cubes and nutritional yeast. Continue to simmer, stirring frequently, until smooth.

Remove from heat and stir in the coconut yogurt.

Carefully stir in the pasta in small batches, folding it into the cheese sauce until well coated.

Tomato Sauce

Makes approximately six jars, 24 ounces each

My grandmother used to make tomato sauce and called it as gravy. She simmered it all night, along with sausage and meatballs, until it took on an almost brown color. I loved it, but it was too fatty and heavy on my system. Over the years I reinvented her recipe and like mine better. The process is different than what you are used to, but it takes on a very rich, deep flavor, that you can adjust with water, like a concentrate. Freeze the leftovers and you will have sauce for several weeks.

1 (28 ounce) can diced tomatoes, drained
4 (6 ounce) cans tomato paste
¼ cup or more raw sugar, to taste
1 Tablespoon dried oregano
Sea salt and pepper to taste
Red pepper flakes, optional

1 (28 ounce) can tomato purée
2 cloves garlic, chopped
1 Tablespoon dried basil
1 Tablespoon dried parsley
Olive oil, as needed
Water, as needed

Blend the diced tomatoes and purée in a blender. Set aside.

In a stock pot sauté garlic in enough olive oil to coat the pan until it begins to brown, about 2-3 minutes. Add more oil to coat the bottom of the pan and add tomato paste.

Reduce heat to low-medium, and stir frequently, adding more oil as needed, to brown the paste. The goal is to make it as dark as possible without burning. This process may require you to add more oil, so keep the bottle handy. Paste should turn dark brick red in about 30 minutes.

Add the blended tomato products, stirring in gradually until well incorporated, and reduce heat. Add your spices and sugar. Simmer about 40 minutes, stirring frequently. Sauce should be very thick, like gravy.

Stir in water to thin the sauce out to your desired texture. You may use several cups in the process, so do not be concerned by the quantity.

Taste sauce to adjust your flavors. If you like the sauce very sweet you can add more sugar. If you want it spicier, add additional red pepper flakes and/or Italian spices as needed.

Once you have it as you wish, cook just until fully heated through and serve.

When cool, you can transfer sauce to jars or freezer safe containers.

Fettuccine Alfredo
Makes 8 servings

This creamy and delicious meal is very rich, so I suggest using this as a side dish, and offsetting the high caloric intake with a large dinner salad.

ooooooooooooooooooooooooooooooooooooooooooooooooooooooooooooooooooooooooooooooooooooo

1 pound gluten-free fettuccine or other pasta
2 cups plain rice milk
1 package Daiya havarti wedge, diced
2 cups shredded Daiya mozzarella cheese
1 cup broccoli florets, cut small
2 Tablespoons water

1 cup Earth Balance soy-free spread
1 Tablespoon nutritional yeast
½ cup plain coconut yogurt
1 cup sliced button mushrooms
2 teaspoons tapioca starch

Bring a large pot of water to a boil. Add fettuccine and cook according to package instructions, adding broccoli florets during the final minute of cooking.

While pasta is cooking, melt Earth Balance over low heat. Stir in rice milk and mushrooms. Simmer 5 minutes.

Stir in cheeses and nutritional yeast, stirring frequently, until melted. Stir in the coconut yogurt and continue to simmer on low.

Combine the tapioca starch and water, stirring to remove any lumps. Add to the cheese sauce and stir well to incorporate.

Remove from heat and cover the pan until the pasta is done.

Drain fettuccine well. Add pasta to sauce, gently tossing to coat. Serve immediately.

Spaghetti and Neatballs

Makes 8 servings

These Neatballs are great substitutes for meatballs, and my husband learned that work great pressed into patties for burgers, or crumbled as a taco filling.

○○

1 pound gluten-free spaghetti
½ pound brown lentils
½ pound portabella mushrooms, diced
1 celery stalk, chopped fine
4 cups vegetable stock
1 teaspoon dried oregano
Sea salt and pepper, to taste
½ cup Daiya shredded mozzarella cheese

1 cups tomato sauce, page 132
1 cup brown rice
½ medium onion, chopped fine
1 teaspoon parsley flakes
1 clove minced garlic
1 teaspoon dried basil
Red pepper flakes, optional
Coconut oil for the pan

Bring stock to a boil, then reduce heat and cover pot. Add lentils and rice and simmer until both are soft, about 45 minutes. Check the liquid frequently and add more stock if necessary.

When ready, add half of the mixture to a food processor, along with the onions, celery, and mushrooms. Process into a thick pulp.

Remove lentils from processor and combine with the rest of the lentil and rice mixture in a large bowl. Add in shredded mozzarella, garlic, oregano, basil, and parsley, along with sea salt and pepper to taste.

Preheat oven to 350°F. Grease a cookie sheet with coconut oil.

Shape mixture into balls, about the size of a golf ball. You can cook the entire mix now or shape and freeze the uncooked extras.

Place balls on cookie sheet on center rack of oven and bake 15 minutes, or until they reach a dark color. Remove from heat, and spoon a small amount of tomato sauce over them. Allow to cool until ready to serve.

Simmer tomato sauce while the other items are cooking. Cover, reduce heat to low, and continue to keep warm until ready to serve.

While these are baking, bring a large stockpot of water to a boil. Add spaghetti, and cook according to package instructions. Drain well and set aside.

Veggie Lasagna

Makes 8 servings

This lasagna is certainly filling enough, but you can use the Neatballs on page 134 as a crumbled filler if you would like more protein and substance.

ooooooooooooooooooooooooooooooooooooooooooooooooooooooooooooooooooooooooooooooooooo

1 (16 ounce) package gluten-free lasagna
¾ cup green bell pepper, diced
3 cloves garlic, minced
2 Tablespoons olive oil
4 cups shredded Daiya mozzarella cheese

1 pound fresh mushrooms, sliced
¾ cup chopped onion
4 cups tomato sauce, page 132
1 teaspoon dried basil
Coconut oil for your pan

Cook the lasagna noodles in a large pot of boiling water for 10 minutes, or until al dente. Rinse with cold water, and drain. Do not overcook, as they will continue to cook in the baking process.

In a large saucepan, cook the mushrooms, green peppers, onion, and garlic in the olive oil. Stir in pasta sauce and basil and bring to a boil. Reduce heat, and simmer 15 minutes. Set aside.

Preheat oven to 350°F.

Spread 1 cup tomato sauce into the bottom of a 9x13 inch baking dish greased with coconut oil. Layer lasagna noodles, then sauce, and then cheese. Repeat layering until you run out of noodles, and top with remaining cheese.

Bake, uncovered on the center rack for 30 minutes, then cover with aluminum and bake an additional 15 minutes.

Let stand 5 minutes before cutting to help it retain its shape.

Caulipasta

Makes 8 servings

This is great served with any of our breads and a salad. If you prefer, substitute broccoli.

1 head cauliflower, broken into florets
1 small onion, diced
1 teaspoon chopped fresh parsley
Sea salt and pepper to taste
1 pound gluten-free pasta of choice

½ cup extra virgin olive oil
2 cloves garlic, minced
¼ teaspoon garlic powder
½ cup Daiya mozzarella cheese
1 cup kalamata olives, pitted

Cook pasta in a large pot of boiling water until al dente, according to the package instructions. Drain well, and transfer back into the pan. Set aside.

Meanwhile, break cauliflower into florets, and steam until you achieve your desired level of tenderness.

Heat olive oil in a large skillet. Add onion and garlic, and sauté until golden.

Stir in cauliflower, sea salt, and pepper, and continue to cook to coat cauliflower with the oil and seasonings for just a few minutes, being careful not to break the florets.

Stir the cauliflower mix into the pasta, folding in gently.

Add kalamata olives and shredded cheese. Cover and remove from heat, allowing to sit for 5 minutes before serving.

Primavera

Makes 6 servings

What I love about primavera is that you can use any seasonal vegetables you have available. This is my favorite combination.

°°

12 ounces gluten-free penne
1 medium zucchini, chopped
½ red bell pepper, julienned
½ cup broccoli florets
¼ cup olive oil, divided
½ Tablespoon lemon juice
1 Tablespoon coconut oil
2 cloves garlic, minced
1/3 cup chopped fresh parsley
1 cup green beans, trimmed and cut in half

1 medium yellow squash, chopped
1 medium carrot, julienned
½ pint cherry or grape tomatoes
½ cup cauliflower florets
Sea salt and pepper, to taste
1 Tablespoon Italian seasoning
¼ large yellow onion, thinly sliced
1/3 cup chopped fresh basil leaves
3 Tablespoons balsamic vinegar
10 asparagus spears, chopped

Preheat oven to 450°F. Line a baking sheet with aluminum foil.

Bring a large pot of water to a boil. Add penne pasta and cook until al dente; drain and place in a large bowl.

While the pasta is cooking, toss all the vegetables except the tomatoes and onions, with 2 Tablespoons olive oil, sea salt, pepper, lemon juice, and Italian seasoning in a large bowl.

Arrange vegetables on the baking sheet, and roast 10 minutes on the center rack, until tender. When done, add to the pasta and fold in gently. Set aside.

Heat remaining olive oil and coconut oil in a large skillet. Stir in the onion, tomatoes, and garlic, and cook until tender.

Mix in the basil, parsley, and balsamic vinegar and heat just a minute or two longer to incorporate the flavors.

Remove from heat and gently toss with roasted vegetables and pasta.

If desired, top with cheese or tomato sauce.

Potato Pasta

Makes 8 servings

Having trouble finding gluten-free pasta in your area? Would you prefer to make your own rather than open a box? I know I do. It is not quite as hard as you may think, and for those who used to enjoy the art of homemade pasta making, this is a real treat. I suggest also experimenting with various gluten-free flours for different flavors and textures. I find this one to be the most versatile, but I have had wonderful results using gluten-free oat flour, amaranth, quinoa, and buckwheat, so have fun! Make extras to freeze for later.

2/3 cup potato flour (not starch)
½ teaspoon sea salt
1 Tablespoon Egg Replacer
1 Tablespoon canola oil

2 Tablespoons tapioca starch
1 teaspoon xanthan gum
¼ cup plain rice milk

Combine rice milk and Egg Replacer. Stir well and set aside.

Combine flour, starches, sea salt and gum. Add oil and prepared Egg Replacer, and stir to create a dough. Knead until you can form a firm ball. If not, add a bit more flour.

Place ball of dough on a board or lightly floured surface and roll out as thin as possible.

You will know you have the right thinness and texture if the dough is tough and although almost transparent, will still handle well.

Slice the noodles into very thin strips, or if using for lasagna, into 1-1/2" x 4" rectangles. The pasta is now ready to cook or to freeze uncooked for later use.

If you are using a pasta maker, please follow the manufacturer's instructions.

Place in freezer safe packaging and date the package. Fresh pasta will last for 3 months in the freezer or 1 week in the refrigerator.

When you are ready to cook the pasta, bring a large pot of lightly salted water to a boil, add 1 tablespoon of oil, and cook for 5 to 10 minutes, depending on the size of your pieces.

Pasta Au Gratin

Makes 8 servings

An easy casserole to whip up for unexpected company, this is hearty, yummy, and crowd pleasing, regardless of the crowd you are feeding.

○○

(1) 15 ounce can kernel corn, including liquid
1 cup gluten-free elbow macaroni, dry
1 cup Daiya shredded cheddar cheese
Coconut oil for your pan

(1) 15 ounce can creamed corn
½ cup Earth Balance soy-free spread
1 package Daiya havarti wedged, cubed
Red pepper flakes, optional, to taste

Preheat oven to 350°F. Grease a into a shallow 1½ quart casserole dish with coconut oil.

Pour kernel corn and liquid, pasta, and half of the shredded cheese and cubes into the dish and stir.

Pour creamed corn slowly over the top of the mixture.

Add remaining cheese, red pepper flakes if using, and dot with Earth Balance.

Cover casserole with an oven safe lid or aluminum foil and bake for 35 minutes on the center rack of the oven.

Remove cover, and bake for an additional 5-10 minutes, or until top is slightly browned and macaroni is tender.

Serve immediately.

Veggie Lo Mein

Makes 4 servings

An easy remake of a classic Chinese favorite, this can be modified to suit your tastes and what vegetables you have on hand.

8 ounces gluten-free linguini
2 cups fresh sliced mushrooms
½ cup sliced red bell peppers
2 cloves garlic, minced
½ cup chopped green onions
1 cup vegetable stock
2 Tablespoons agave nectar

3 Tablespoons coconut oil
1 cup shredded carrots
1 medium onion, chopped
1 cup broccoli florets
1 Tablespoon cornstarch
¼ cup coconut aminos
1 teaspoon grated fresh ginger

Bring a large pot of water to a boil. Add noodles and cook according to package instructions. One minute before done, drop broccoli in the pot for the last minute of cooking time. Drain and set aside.

Heat oil in a large wok or pan. Fry the mushrooms, green onions, carrots, peppers, onion, and garlic until tender with the garlic and ginger. Stir fry for 5 minutes, until crisp.

Mix cornstarch and stock together in a small bowl and add to stir fry. Continue to simmer until sauce thickens. Stir in coconut aminos and agave nectar. Add cooked spaghetti, and toss gently to combine.

Pad Thai

Makes 4 servings

A delicious and safe remake that is free from wheat, peanuts, and seafood products, this Pad Thai is tasty and fun to make.

12 ounces thick rice noodles
1 Tablespoon white wine vinegar
3 Tablespoons raw sugar
½ teaspoon curry powder
¼ cup sunflower seeds
½ cup shredded carrots
1 clove of garlic, minced

2 Tablespoons coconut oil
2 Tablespoons coconut aminos
¼ teaspoon crushed red pepper
2 cups bean sprouts
3 green onions, chopped
½ cup shredded green cabbage
¼ teaspoon ginger powder

Cook rice noodles according to package instructions. Drain and set aside.

Heat coconut oil in a wok or large heavy skillet over medium-high heat. Add all vegetables other than bean sprouts, as well as the vinegar, curry powder, ginger, garlic, coconut aminos, sugar, and red pepper flakes. Stir fry until tender, about 5 minutes.

Mix in noodles and continue to cook to blend the flavors, about 3 minutes, stirring carefully to avoid breaking the noodles.

Top with bean sprouts and sunflower seeds just before serving.

Vegetables and Potatoes

Going gluten-free, nut-free, and soy-free while being vegan really helped me create some flavorful and interesting vegetable and potato meals. Since I love variety, I usually serve one of these with a soup, salad, appetizer, and bread, and feel like I have really eaten a hearty, filling, nutritious meal.

Saag

Makes 4 Servings

Saag is a potato Curry with a combination of bitter and mild greens. Any combination of seasonal greens will work. I personally prefer spinach with turnip greens, which is what I offer here.

○○

½ cup coconut oil
4 medium russet potatoes, peeled and quartered
2 Tablespoons turmeric
1 pound chopped fresh spinach leaves
1 teaspoon coriander
1 teaspoon black pepper

2 teaspoons cumin seed
2 cloves garlic, minced
1 pound chopped turnip greens
1 teaspoon cumin
1 teaspoon sea salt
Red pepper flakes to taste

In a large skillet, melt coconut oil over medium-high heat. Cook cumin seed, garlic, and turmeric until fragrant, about 2 minutes.

Add potatoes and reduce heat. Cook for 15 minutes, stirring frequently.

Stir in the greens and spinach a little at a time, until all greens have been added and begin to wilt.

Stir in the cumin, coriander, red pepper flakes, sea salt and pepper. Cover; reduce heat and simmer until potatoes are tender, about 10 minutes, adding a small amount of water if needed.

Serve over Biryani, page 120 with chapati, 55, on the side.

Eggplant Parmesan

Makes 4 Servings

One of my favorite comfort foods from childhood, this dish still is what I opt for most on a holiday. You can omit the breading if you want to, but I really prefer it with bread crumbs.

2 medium eggplants, peeled and thinly sliced
¼ cup water
4 cups gluten-free bread crumbs
16 ounces Daiya shredded mozzarella cheese, divided
½ teaspoon oregano
½ teaspoon pepper

1 Tablespoon Egg Replacer
½ cup plain rice milk
6 cups tomato sauce, page 132
½ teaspoon dried basil
½ teaspoon sea salt
½ teaspoon parsley flakes

Preheat oven to 425°F. Grease two cookie sheets with coconut oil and set aside.

Combine bread crumbs and spices together in a large bowl. Set aside.

Prepare Egg Replacer with water and stir well in a medium sized bowl. Add rice milk, and dip eggplant slices in mixture, then into the seasoned bread crumbs.

Place in a single layer on a baking sheet. Bake for 5 minutes on each side to brown. Remove from heat and allow to cool so the bread crumbs are set.

In a 9x13 inch baking dish, spread a small amount of tomato sauce on the bottom. Place a layer of eggplant slices on top.

Sprinkle with mozzarella and sauce, and repeat with remaining ingredients, layering eggplant, sauce, and cheese, ending with cheese on the top layer.

Cover pan with aluminum foil, reduce heat to 350°F, and bake for 35 minutes.

Remove aluminum and bake 10 minutes more.

Allow pan to sit for 5 minutes before serving.

Potatoes Au Gratin

Makes 4 Servings

This makes a great side dish, or with a bit of broccoli or other veggie, a main course.

○○○

4 large potatoes, peeled and sliced ¼ inch
Coconut oil for greasing the pan
½ teaspoon sea salt
1½ cups Daiya shredded cheddar cheese
3 Tablespoons Earth Balance soy-free spread

1 medium onion, sliced into rings
3 Tablespoons Free State flour, page 11
2 cups plain rice milk
¼ teaspoon paprika
¼ teaspoon black pepper

Preheat oven to 400°F. Grease a 1 quart casserole dish with coconut oil. Set aside.

Place potatoes and onions in a large bowl. Set aside.

In a medium saucepan, melt Earth Balance over medium heat. Mix in the flour, sea salt, pepper, and paprika, and stir constantly for one minute to make a paste.

Stir in the milk, reduce heat, and cook until mixture has thickened.

Stir in the cheese in small batches, stirring frequently until you have a smooth cheese sauce.

Pour cheese over the potatoes and onions, and stir carefully to coat.

Transfer to the casserole dish and cover with aluminum foil or an oven safe lid.

Bake for 35 minutes on the center rack of the oven, remove cover, and continue to bake another 10 minutes, or until the potatoes are tender but still slightly firm.

Mashed Sweet Potato Bake

Makes 4 Servings

A more nutritious version of mashed potatoes, sweet potatoes are much higher in Vitamins A and C, as well as Resistant Starch (RS) which is currently being identified as a key to help them with Diabetes and obesity manage blood sugar.

4 large sweet potatoes, peeled, cut in quarters
½ cup Earth Balance soy-free spread
½ cup shredded Daiya cheddar cheese
5 carrots, chopped

¼ cup plain coconut milk
1 Tablespoon diced onion
Sea salt and pepper to taste
1 Tablespoon coconut oil

Bring a large pot of sea salted water to a boil. Add sweet potatoes and carrots, and cook until tender but still firm, about 20 minutes. Drain and mash.

Mix in Earth Balance, finely chopped onion and ¼ cup of the Daiya cheese. Season with sea salt and pepper to taste; set aside.

Preheat oven to 375°F.

Spread the mashed sweet potato carrot mix on the bottom of a greased 2 quart casserole dish. Next, spread a layer of mashed carrots. Sprinkle with remaining shredded cheese.

Bake on the center rack, covered, for 20 minutes, or until golden brown.

Mushroom Cacciatore

Makes 4 Servings

A versatile mushroom dish that can be used as a pasta or rice topping, or as a side dish.

8 portabella mushroom caps, stems removed
1 teaspoon dried basil
1 teaspoon agave nectar
1 cup chopped yellow onion
1 clove garlic, minced
Cooked rice or pasta, optional
Coconut oil for greasing pan
2 cups tomato sauce, page 132

4 Tablespoons olive oil
1 teaspoon dried oregano
1 cup Free State flour, page 11
1 (28 ounce) can tomato purée
Sea salt pepper to taste
Bowl of rice milk for dipping
Red pepper flakes, optional

Cut mushrooms in half. Add oil to a large skillet, and cook for 5 minutes. Remove from heat and allow to cool.

Mix together the flour, sea salt and pepper to make seasoned flour.

Preheat oven to 350°F. Grease a cookie sheet with coconut oil. Set aside.

Dip each mushroom half in a shallow bowl of rice milk, then in flour mixture until all pieces are coated. Place on cookie sheet when done. Repeat until all are coated.

Bake mushrooms on the center rack of the oven for 6 minutes, flip pieces, and bake another 6 minutes, or until they begin to brown.

While the mushrooms bake, sauté onions and garlic in a large skillet in a little bit of oil, 3-5 minutes, until the onions begin to brown.

In a large bowl, combine remaining ingredients and add to onions and garlic. Add mushroom slices to skillet. Cover and reduce heat, simmering for 30 minutes. Serve hot.

Baked Spaghetti Squash

Makes 4 Servings

Spaghetti squash has all the fun and flair of real pasta, minus the heaviness.

2 Tablespoons olive oil
1 clove garlic, minced
¾ cup shredded Daiya mozzarella cheese
2 Tablespoons chopped fresh basil
1 medium spaghetti squash, halved lengthwise and seeded

1 small onion, chopped
1½ cups tomatoes, diced
¼ cup sliced black olives
Coconut oil for the pan

Preheat oven to 350°F. Lightly grease a baking sheet with coconut oil. Set aside.

Cut squash in half and remove the seeds and stringy matter. Place cut sides down on the prepared baking sheet, and bake 30 minutes, or until a sharp knife can be inserted with only a little resistance.

Remove squash from oven, and set aside to cool.

Meanwhile, heat olive oil in a skillet over medium heat. Sauté onion and garlic until the onions become tender, about 5 minutes.

Stir in the tomatoes and olives, and cook only until tomatoes are warm.

Use a fork to loosen the spaghetti squash strings and seeds from the shells. Discard. Scrap out the squash and place in a medium bowl.

Toss with cooked tomatoes, top with basil and cheese, and serve warm.

Greek Style Green Beans

Makes 4 Servings

One of my favorite ways to serve green beans, I regularly have this as a main course. It is super easy to make, and simmers up without much need to pay attention to it.

6 cups vegetable stock
1 pound fresh green beans, trimmed
2 cans (14.5 ounce) whole peeled potatoes, drained
1 teaspoon black pepper

3 cups tomato sauce, page 132
1 large onion, chopped
1 Tablespoon sea salt
1 Tablespoon garlic powder

Combine all ingredients, bring to a boil, then cover and simmer over low heat, about 1 hour.

Add the potatoes and continue to simmer for 30 minutes more, or until they can be easily pierced with a fork.

Squash Curry

You can add beans to this simple meal if you wish. I enjoy this with soup, chapatti, and served over rice.

○○

¼ cup coconut oil

1 Tablespoon curry powder

2/3 cup vegetable stock

1 (10 ounce) bag fresh spinach leaves

1 Tablespoon fresh cilantro

1 teaspoon tapioca starch

1 pound of kabocha (buttercup) acorn, or other winter squash, peeled and cubed

1 large onion, chopped

2 cups plain coconut milk

Sea salt and pepper to taste

1 Tablespoon fresh cilantro

1 teaspoon mustard powder

2 Tablespoons water

Cook the onion in the coconut oil over medium heat until it begins to brown, about 5-10 minutes.

Stir in the mustard powder and curry powder, and cook for 2 minutes longer. Add the coconut milk, water, and squash. Bring to a boil over high heat, then reduce heat to medium-low, cover, and simmer until the squash is tender, about 15-20 minutes.

Season to taste with sea salt and pepper, then stir in the spinach and cilantro. Simmer a few more minutes until spinach is wilted.

Stir the water into the tapioca starch. Gently fold into the mix to thicken the sauce, and simmer for 2 minutes.

Serve alone or over rice.

Brussels Pomodoro

Makes 4 Servings

You can add white beans to increase the protein, but I prefer to serve this as a side dish with Eggplant Parmesan, page 144 or one of our pasta dishes.

○○

3 cups tomato juice
2 Tablespoons olive oil
1 teaspoon dried oregano
3 large tomatoes, diced

1 pound Brussels sprouts, trimmed
2 cloves garlic, minced
Sea salt and pepper to taste
1 teaspoon dried basil

Bring the tomato juice to a boil in a large saucepan. Add Brussels sprouts and cook for 5 to 7 minutes, until slightly firm.

Drain, and rinse with cold water. Discard the tomato juice. Allow sprouts to cool before handling.

Slice the sprouts in half, and set aside.

Heat one tablespoon of oil in a large skillet over medium heat. Add the garlic and tomatoes; cook and stir for about 5 minutes.

Add the remaining oil and Brussels sprouts, oregano, and basil. Reduce the heat to medium-low and cook, stirring frequently until the sprouts are well coated with the spices, about 5 minutes more.

Season with sea salt and pepper just before serving.

Stewed Zucchini

Makes 4 Servings

I love to serve this on a bed of spaghetti squash.

2 Tablespoons olive oil
2 cloves garlic, minced
2 (14 ounce) cans stewed tomatoes
1 cup Daiya shredded cheddar cheese

½ small onion, sliced thinly
8 zucchini, sliced ¼ -inch thick
Sea salt and pepper to taste
Spaghetti squash, optional

Heat the olive oil in a saucepan over medium heat; cook the onion and garlic in the hot oil until soft, about 5 minutes.

Add the zucchini slices and stewed tomatoes and stir gently. Cover and cook until the zucchini is tender, 8 to 10 minutes.

Remove from heat, season with sea salt, and add the cheddar cheese; allow to sit until the cheese has melted.

Serve on a bed of cooked spaghetti squash, rice, pasta, or with chapati.

Potato Enchiladas

Makes 4 Servings

This recipe was created in the spirit of trying to make a good use of leftovers. To make fresh, you can follow the recipe below, and time it so that the potatoes are cooking at the same time as the vegetables are roasting to get you out of the kitchen faster.

○○

1 head broccoli, cut into small florets
3 small zucchini, diced
¼ cup coconut oil
½ cup Earth Balance soy-free spread, divided
10 medium red potatoes
¼ cup plain coconut yogurt
3 cups enchilada sauce of choice
8 ounces Daiya shredded cheddar cheese

8 ounces sliced mushrooms
2 cups diced carrots
Sea salt and pepper to taste
1½ cups plain rice milk
8 gluten-free corn tortillas
1 teaspoon onion powder
Sea salt and pepper, to taste
1 Tablespoon chili powder

Preheat oven to 425°F. Grease a cookie sheet with coconut oil.

In a large mixing bowl, combine broccoli, mushrooms, zucchini, and carrots. Season with sea salt, pepper, and paprika. Spread vegetables in a single layer in a shallow baking dish. Dot with additional coconut oil. Roast vegetables for 30 minutes; stir halfway through their cooking time.

While the vegetables roast, make the mashed potatoes.

Fill a large pot with water. Add potatoes. Bring to a boil, and simmer to boil until potatoes are soft, about 20 minutes or so. Drain.

Fill pot with cold water, and place potatoes into the cold water for 5 minutes, to cool. Drain again, and remove skins. Transfer potatoes to a large bowl. Mash potatoes, adding sea salt and pepper, onion powder, and gradually add Earth Balance, coconut yogurt, and rice milk until you achieve the right consistency. You may not need all the rice milk or Earth Balance. Set aside.

When the vegetables are finished cooking, remove from the oven, and reduce oven temperature to 350°F. Stir the roasted vegetables into the mashed potatoes. Set aside.Add enchilada sauce to a large bowl. Set aside.

In a dry skillet over medium heat, quickly heat each tortilla on both sides to make pliable. Dip the tortillas in enchilada sauce. Put a large spoonful of mixture into the center of each tortilla. Top mixture with about 1 to 2 tablespoons cheese, and roll tortillas. Place seam-side down in a 9x13 inch baking dish. Pour extra sauce over top, and sprinkle with remaining cheese. Bake covered on the center rack for 30 minutes, or until the enchiladas are heated through. Allow to sit for 5 minutes before serving to help keep them intact.

Fajitas

Makes 4 Servings

What I love about this recipe is that it is a traditional Mexican meal that does not scream gluten-free, vegan, or allergy restricted.

8 chapati, page 53
1 small red onion, thinly sliced
1 red bell pepper, julienned
1 medium yellow squash, julienned
1 cup cauliflower florets, cut small
1 teaspoon chili powder
¼ teaspoon cayenne pepper
½ cup guacamole, page 49
1 cup shredded Daiya pepperjack cheese

2 Tablespoons coconut oil
1 green bell pepper, julienned
1 teaspoon minced garlic
1 medium zucchini, julienned
1 cup broccoli florets, cut small
1 teaspoon ground cumin
½ teaspoon sea salt
½ cup salsa, page 49
Beans and rice, optional

In skillet, heat oil over medium heat. Add onions, red and green peppers, and garlic; stir to coat with oil. Cover, reduce heat to medium, and cook for 5 minutes.

Add cauliflower, broccoli, zucchini, and squash into vegetables. Stir in chili powder, cumin, cayenne and sea salt. Cover, and cook an additional 5 minutes.

Spoon vegetable mixture evenly down the centers of chapati, and sprinkle with cheese.

Top with salsa and guacamole, and serve with your choice of beans and rice.

US Recipe Measurement Conversions

Liquids, Herbs, and Spices Converted

Liquids can be converted to liters or milliliters with the following table. Small volumes (less than about 1 fluid ounce or 2 tablespoons) of ingredients such as salt, herbs, spices, baking powder, etc. should also be converted with this table.

American	Metric
1 teaspoon	5 mL
1 tablespoon *or* 1/2 fluid ounce	15 mL
1 fluid ounce *or* 1/8 cup	30 mL
1/4 cup *or* 2 fluid ounces	60 mL
1/3 cup	80 mL
1/2 cup *or* 4 fluid ounces	120 mL
2/3 cup	160 mL
3/4 cup *or* 6 fluid ounces	180 mL
1 cup *or* 8 fluid ounces *or* half a pint	240 mL
1 1/2 cups *or* 12 fluid ounces	350 mL
2 cups *or* 1 pint *or* 16 fluid ounces	475 mL
3 cups *or* 1 1/2 pints	700 mL
4 cups *or* 2 pints *or* 1 quart	950 mL
4 quarts *or* 1 gallon	3.8 L

Note: In cases where higher precision is not justified, it may be convenient to round these conversions off as follows:
  1 cup = 250 mL
  1 pint = 500 mL
  1 quart = 1 L
  1 gallon = 4 L

Weights

American	Metric
1 ounce	28 g
4 ounces *or* ¼ pound	113 g
1/3 pound	150 g
8 ounces *or* ½ pound	230 g
2/3 pound	300 g
12 ounces *or* ¾ pound	340 g
1 pound *or* 16 ounces	450 g
2 pounds	900 g

Lengths

Keep in mind that 1 cm = 10 mm

American	Metric
1/8 inch	3 mm
1/4 inch	6 mm
1/2 inch	13 mm
3/4 inch	19 mm
1 inch	2.5 cm
2 inches	5 cm
3 inches	7.6 cm
4 inches	10 cm
5 inches	13 cm
6 inches	15 cm
7 inches	18 cm
8 inches	20 cm
9 inches	23 cm
10 inches	25 cm
11 inches	28 cm
12 inches *or* 1 foot	30 cm

Temperature: Fahrenheit to Celsius

Here is a quick list of the most common temperatures

300°F	148°C
325°F	162°C
350°F	176°C
375°F	190°C
400°F	204°C
425°F	218°C
450°F	232°C

About the Author

Upon graduating magna cum laude with a degree in English, Dawn Hamilton decided to focus on personal healing before embarking on her career goals. During that time, she immersed herself in the study of nutritional and holistic healing.

After discovering her lifelong obesity and other chronic health ailments were the result of food sensitivities, she changed her diet and mindset. Without starvation or excessive exercise she lost over 170 pounds which she has successfully maintained for over fifteen years.

Since then, Dawn has earned certification as a Clinical Nutritionist, Holistic Health Practitioner, and Doctor of Naturopathy. She is a popular wellness coach who has assisted over 7,000 clients worldwide learn awareness of food's effect on the body.

Hamilton has been featured on radio shows, wellness blogs, newspapers, and is a highly sought out public speaker. In addition to this book, she is the author of *Free State Bakery's Nothing to Sneeze At*.

Recipe Index

Chapter headings in bold italics

CPSIA information can be obtained
at www.ICGtesting.com
Printed in the USA
BVHW011059240319
543530BV00018B/586/P

9 781478 274858